To Debbie
Best Wishes
John Emerald.

Susan Emerald

28th NOV 09

John and Susan Emerald came together in late 2006.

John has three children from his previous marriage, and two children with Susan.

Both are Spiritualist Mediums, but equally have other professions.

For John this is accountancy, and for Susan, a therapeutic role in child protection.

Susan also is a trained natural Nutritionist, and a great follower of Homeopathy. Susan has written articles for magazines, such as She, Woman and Elle and was a regular columnist for Primary Times, giving advice on health and parenting.

John loves to write poetry, short stories, and for several years was a weekly columnist for Psychic News.

JIMMY JONES

John & Susan Emerald

JIMMY JONES

Vanguard Press

VANGUARD PAPERBACK

© Copyright 2009
John & Susan Emerald

The right of John & Susan Emerald to be identified as authors of this work has been asserted by them in accordance with the
Copyright, Designs and Patents Act 1988.

All Rights Reserved

No reproduction, copy or transmission of this publication
may be made without written permission.
No paragraph of this publication may be reproduced,
copied or transmitted save with the written permission of the publisher, or
in accordance with the provisions
of the Copyright Act 1956 (as amended).

Any person who commits any unauthorised act in relation to
this publication may be liable to criminal
prosecution and civil claims for damages.

The views expressed within this book are those of the Spirit people, and are not necessarily the views of John and Susan Emerald.

A CIP catalogue record for this title is
available from the British Library.

ISBN 978 184386 582 7

*Vanguard Press is an imprint of
Pegasus Elliot MacKenzie Publishers Ltd.*
www.pegasuspublishers.com

First Published in 2009

**Vanguard Press
Sheraton House Castle Park
Cambridge England**

Printed & Bound in Great Britain

We dedicate *Jimmy Jones,*
to Hannah, Natasha, Matthew, Sara and Martin,
our beloved children.

Acknowledgements

Our grateful thanks to Ian, Gabriel, Cathy, Ted and Ken, all our family and friends, and the publishing team.

Our heartfelt thanks to our Spirit friends, without whose direction none of this would have been possible.

Foreword

Ladies and Gentlemen, those of you reading this book may find it rather strange that the foreword is written by a gentleman who has been dead for many, many years. I can understand how difficult a concept that may be for you to grasp, yet it is the truth.

We come from the world of Spirit to address you in this book, to make you aware not only of our continued existence but equally to show you, and make you aware of what others are doing on your earthly plain of existence, and that you should be aware of things that are sometimes done in your name.

Some things that are done are by those you would call terrorists who believe very passionately in what they are doing, but who by their very actions, undermine the society that you strive to maintain, love and support. I do hope that this book will be of an inspiration to you and that it may find you searching for more answers than you have found already. I look forward, if it be the divine spirit's will, that I can address you on other occasions.
Yours,
Sir Arthur Conan Doyle

Contents

1 JIMMY JONES 17

2 WINSTON CHURCHILL 22

3 THE DUKE OF WINDSOR 27

4 DODI AL FAYED 31

5 PRINCESS DIANA 47

6 JIMMY AND DIANA 54

7 TERRORISTS AND LANDMINES 72

8 DIANA'S RECOVERY 84

9 NEW YEAR, NEW CONVERSATION 97

10 GHANDI & VLADIMIR 103

11 ALEXANDER AND GHANDI 115

12 DIANA AND VLADIMIR 134

13 DODI AND WINSTON 145

1 JIMMY JONES

"Hi, I'm Jimmy Jones, and I've been asked to come and help you!" Jimmy said to John.

"Help me?" I answered.

"Yes!" said the bright and cheery young man in military uniform.

I took time to look at Jimmy, he looked to be in his early twenties, about 5'8" in height, with a lean but firm build.

"Sorry Jimmy, you said help me? Help me to do what exactly?"

"I've come as your personal guide, a sort of intermediary. My job is to introduce you to several people from what you understand as the Spirit world. What we'd like you to do, is faithfully record all that is said to you."

"Sounds interesting Jimmy, tell me more," I said. "I mean are you asking me to write some sort of book, and if so, what is the purpose?"

"The purpose will become clear as time goes by, but believe me this book will be of interest to many people. Some will try to rubbish it, others will be in awe, and the majority will have something to think about."

Jimmy stood there smiling at me; I could tell that he knew my interest had stirred. Throwing caution to the wind I said, "Ok Jimmy, I'll do it!"

I wondered if Jimmy really appreciated who he was taking on, after all I'm not known as having a 'yes sir' kind of personality. I may well be accepting of the fact that life continues after so called death, but I'm not so gullible to accept everything I'm being told as being unquestionable. There and then Jimmy and I began to have a chat, well mostly it was me asking questions, and Jimmy patiently providing me with answers.

I could see from Jimmy's uniform that he was a private serving in the army, he told me that he used to be a 'sapper', for me the word sapper was one I had heard before but wasn't entirely certain what it meant. Before I could even ask the question, Jimmy said "an engineer!"

Somehow knowing my questions before I could speak them Jimmy continued. "I was 22 when I was killed, I was part of the Lancashire regiment, died in no-man's-land between the two fronts, trying to lay a tread board over the top of some barbed wire so our troops could cross. I'd just laid it down, when I was machine-gunned.

"World War One?" I asked.

Jimmy smiled, "Yes, that's right, World War One, the Battle of the Somme."

I was intrigued by this conversation, some questions answered, others begging to be asked. Sadly I had to end our conversation as I had an appointment elsewhere. "Sorry Jimmy, I have to go now." Again Jimmy gave me that knowing smile, "No problem, call me when you want to chat some more." He gave a cheery wave and then just faded from view.

In the cool light of day I had time to reflect on Jimmy's evidence, I also had a golden opportunity to check his story and see if I could verify or otherwise his testimony. My first point of reference was of course the great World Wide Web. Searching for a Jimmy or James Jones was not going to be an easy task. After all the surname of Jones has to be one of the most common surnames in Britain.

No-one could have been more surprised than me to find details about Jimmy, including his mother and father's names along with his last known address, presumably the family home. I decided it was time to find out more.

So one sunny Sunday morning, I got up knowing somehow that I needed to go to a country park some distance from home. I didn't know why, but I had a clear vision of a single oak tree standing just away from the rest of a group of trees, I could see that the tree would offer plenty of shade and also would provide very quiet surroundings. Arriving at the country park, one I had never bothered to visit before, I was greeted with the oak tree and its surroundings as had been shown to me. Being suitably situated it seemed an ideal time to ask Jimmy to come and see me again.

Almost as quickly as I could make my request for Jimmy to come and see me, he was there, talking to me as clear as crystal.

"Hi," he said

"Hi Jimmy," I replied, "So we meet again!"

"Glad to see you checked up on me, it's good that you check what you have been told," said Jimmy.

It was my turn to smile; I knew somehow that I didn't need to speak. It was as if we both understood each other, and where we were both coming from. When Jimmy had stood in front of me on that very first occasion, I sensed immediately that this was someone who was not only a good communicator, he was someone who came across as an honest and genuinely amicable gentleman.

Still I had questions relating to what he had told me previously. "Jimmy?" I asked, "You told me that you were a sapper, an engineer, yet the records show you as being a fusilier, why the discrepancy?"

Jimmy once again gave me his cheeky smile. "I wondered when you would pick up on that. You're quite correct I was a fusilier, however, as these things happen in war, our own engineer was gunned down, and us soldiers had to draw straws as to who would take his place and lay down the duck board. I was the unlucky one, pulling the shortest straw it was me who had to go over the top, to lay the board across the wire."

I was still intrigued as to why Jimmy had quite deliberately given me information, which on first inspection seemed to be quite incorrect. Although, being fair, he had clarified the information when challenged. "Let's just say that as well as bringing others to talk to you, part of the work here is to also help others understand the difficulties connected to Spirit communication," said Jimmy in his usual cheery manner. I understood exactly what Jimmy meant, as a demonstrator of Spirit communication and teacher of it; I recognised and understood the importance of checking the evidence with the Spirit communicator.

My curiosity was drawn to these other communicators Jimmy had referred to in our first conversation. Briefly I reflected on some wonderful experiences I had taken part in where I had been used as a transfiguration medium. Let me explain what I mean by transfiguration. Transfiguration is where the face of a spirit can be physically seen to appear over or just in front of the face of the medium.

The medium and sitters present supply the material used to create this phenomena, combined with material supplied by the workers in the spirit realms. Getting back to these previous experiences, I am reliably informed that the faces of both the late Prime Minister Sir Winston Churchill, and the well-known author and Spiritualist Sir Arthur Conan Doyle had been seen to transfigure over my face. I quietly wondered if maybe these two gentlemen would be party to our up coming conversations.

With his usual knowing look, Jimmy said, "But of course, do you not realise by now that this is all part of the plan?" They say ignorance is bliss, and quite honestly I hadn't thought that there was some greater purpose in these manifestations other than maybe to help continue to offer solid evidence of survival after so called death. In fact I had been deeply surprised that characters of such earthly prominence should choose to work with me. Then I smiled as I remembered a comment spoken to me by a spirit communicator on an earlier occasion. "We have to use the instruments we have at our disposal, we can't always pick and choose."

That single comment has helped me on many occasions when talking to people in spirit who were known as celebrities on the earth plane. Many people have asked me before, as to why this person or that person has chosen to speak to me even when there has been no blood relative present. I think the answer to this is much simpler and easier to understand than the ridiculous assertions by many in orthodox religions who claim we contact 'evil' spirits. In the course of my life I have worked in various locations and have been employed by very varied businesses. As a result of this I have come into contact with various celebrities, politicians and members of royal families, as well as many more ordinary folk. Many of these people I had never met before in my life. However, on many occasions on meeting such individuals I have been engaged in interesting conversations with many of them. In short celebrities are no different from you or me, the difference being that they have for whatever reason been placed under the media spotlight. Celebrities often use their influence to highlight issues of importance, such as famines, landmines, cancer and the list goes on. I was soon to have a chat with a very famous man, who had come back to talk to me, his name as he was known on earth was Sir Winston Churchill.

2 WINSTON CHURCHILL

So much has been written about Sir Winston Churchill and his life here on earth, that I did wonder what on earth he could say to me that wasn't already known about. However, the revelations he gave me in our various conversations did indeed raise my eyebrows. When I was first introduced to Winston and had my first conversation, I was in the depths of depression, and feeling very sorry for myself. Winston stood before me, much as I remember seeing him in old newsreel footage. He was smartly dressed, with a walking cane. He stood there in silence as if he was somehow weighing me up. Then this faintest of smiles broke across his face and he spoke. "Young man, pull yourself together, you have much to do and we don't have time to waste!" Winston continued "I suffered from depression just like you are now but you have to learn to control 'it' and not let 'it' control you."

Suitably put straight I decided that now was as good a time as any to start to try and gain some control back into my life. At first my questioning was hesitant, after all who was I to be in a situation where I could chat with one of the greatest characters from British history?

"How should I address you?" I asked.

With no hesitation his reply was given, "Well when on earth I would have insisted on being called 'Sir', however, you can call me anything you like as long as it's not Winnie!"

"In that case Sir," I replied, "I will call you Winston."

"Good," said Winston, "Let's get on with it shall we?"

In history lessons, books and television documentaries I have seen over the years regarding Winston Churchill, nothing I had seen or read gave me any real indication as to his personality. In retrospect I should have known that a leader like Winston would have had very little time for idle gossip or friendly chit chat. Winston was, and I should say remains, a man of action. Not a man to mince his words, and I suspected that comments both positive and negative would have been brief and to the point.

There were so many things I wanted to ask Winston, it was hard to know where to start. However; struggling, as I was with depression, it seemed appropriate to ask questions about how he coped with his 'black dog' as he termed his depression.

Winston's response was "In truth, I struggled, sometimes I won, and sometimes I just had to just keep trying to win!"

"So how did you come to term your depression as your 'black dog'?"

"A faithful dog follows its master, I perceived my depression as a black dog that was with me all the time. Just like a dog I needed to be aware of when it was misbehaving. As the master of the dog I had to train it to behave when it stepped out of line."

The simple answer made a great deal of sense. The illness of depression affects you as an individual; by perceiving it as a separate thing it was a way of stepping back and looking at how you were dealing with the illness. The symbolic presence of a dog was a great way of visualising and crucially managing the illness. I decided that I had my own black dog, and I just needed to train it well!

All of a sudden I felt rather silly. Here was I, being given a golden opportunity to talk to one of the most famous men in British and world history, taking up time asking questions about depression.

Bringing me back on track, as it were, Winston said, "Young man, I have much to tell you along with others, and this all needs to be put down in writing before March 2007."

"Why before March 2007?" I asked.

"There will be further evidence brought to light at that time that will corroborate much of what I have to tell you."

Winston was clearly in the driving seat now, I was still ready to interject and cross-examine his statements, but I decided to do as asked. I sat and waited for Winston to tell me his story which he needed so desperately to have put to paper.

"In June 1940 Britain stood on the brink of being invaded. At the time it was truly our darkest hour. Plans were made, some noted and recorded, others were deemed too important for a written document to evidence existence of a plan or group. In war, desperate times call for desperate measures!"

Winston paused, I felt I was expected to interject so said "What are you trying to tell me?"

"Just bear with me and I shall explain. As I said, Britain stood on the verge of imminent invasion. All our intelligence pointed to a full-scale invasion. With only our own armed forces to fight off such an attempt, we had to think the unthinkable. The unthinkable was of course the way we would continue to fight should our territories be totally overrun. We also knew that the Nazi leadership would predict that we would set up a form of resistance organisation, which would use guerrilla tactics to undermine the occupying forces. We went one better than that, there was the formal set up of such a group, suitably mentioned in top-secret documents. The coup de grâce was the completely secret formation of a second group. The second group had no name, but was made up of people we called 'sleepers'. A sleeper would be recruited by another sleeper, people they knew they could trust. They would lie dormant until such time as the official organisation was no longer workable, by either breach of security or being broken apart by the invading forces."

Winston paused and I sat for some time considering all that he had said. My mind was in a whirl quickly I asked to cross-examine some of the information he had given me.

"So this second unnamed group had what objectives?"

"They had the twin objectives of protecting King and country!" he replied.

Suddenly I felt uneasy, I had this feeling that there was more to this second group. It was apparent though that at this point Winston had no wish to elaborate further. I decided however to continue with getting the background information.

"How would they achieve these objectives?" I enquired.

Winston smiled and said simply "By any means possible."

I had to smile to myself, and the old saying 'ask a foolish question' seemed to buzz around my head. Trying to redeem myself I asked, "So how would this unnamed group be disbanded after the war was concluded?"

Instantly came the reply, "Simple enough, as we were doing with our friends in the resistance groups overseas, a simple phrase would be broadcast, to signal the disbanding of this group."

"So this group were effectively disbanded when the war finished?" I queried.

"Yes, officially disbanded, however…." Winston paused and then continued. "It appears that a small number continued to collaborate together."

Stunned by what Winston had told me I interjected " "Continued to collaborate together? After the disbandment? Why?"

"It would appear that some considered that there was an ongoing threat to King and country, so to protect both, some continued in secrecy."

"Was there any intelligence to suggest this at the time?" I asked.

"There was intelligence to tell us certain activities were being undertaken, however, those involved were clever enough to implicate other terrorist groups," replied Winston.

The implications of what I was being told were astounding. I had a question bouncing around in my head but I was reluctant to voice it. However coming so far now was not the time to hold back. "This group, are they still in existence in some form or other?" I tentatively queried.

In a one word answer came the reply "Yes!"

Winston stood before me, immaculately dressed, in a long black overcoat, hat and walking stick, a small grin on his face. "Young man, that is all I have to tell you for now, but if you need to ask anything else then just call."

With that comment Winston turned and walked briskly away obviously intent on pursuing some other important activity.

3 THE DUKE OF WINDSOR

It was a brief minute or two that I sat there alone after Winston's parting words. In truth I was still trying to absorb all that had been said to me. It sounded like the workings of a fiction novel, however, I could not deny the fact that I had been speaking to a former Prime Minister, whose appearance and voice was instantly recognisable. However, what I had been told left me feeling uneasy.*** Whilst my mind wandered and pondered my conversation with Winston, the equally recognisable, cheery greeting of Jimmy Jones, disturbed my thinking.

"Hello," he said in his truly friendly and warm manner. "That was a turn up for the books eh?" he stated.

"You're right there Jimmy, my head is still reeling from it all."

Jimmy chuckled, and I waited for him to share his thoughts.

"You haven't heard the best of it yet!" he exclaimed.

Not feeling that I wanted to know anything that could be more shocking or disturbing, I decided not to ask the obvious question of "well what is that then?" Silence at this point was my preferred stance. Knowing my thoughts as ever Jimmy said "Well the best way for you to find out more about all this, is for me to introduce someone you have spoken to before, his name is David, otherwise known as the Duke of Windsor."

It is true that I had spoken to David on previous occasions, and it brought back to me the first occasion when he had come from spirit to talk to me. It was many years ago, when I was sitting to develop my mediumship with a lovely medium called Audrey

Terris. My first contact was clairaudient (hearing only) I heard a man's voice, very well spoken who introduced himself to me as 'David'. As the communication progressed David showed himself to me. I was puzzled at the time as to why someone so famous would come to me to talk. It was explained to me later, that Audrey had conducted a sitting with ladies in waiting from one of the royal houses. David had communicated then, and as a result of that connection, continued to make his presence felt in Audrey's circle.

David stood, patiently waiting for my attention. I felt like a schoolchild who had been selected to hand a gift to a distinguished visitor, and so I greeted David with a somewhat inappropriate but simple greeting of "Hello."

David smiled; he seemed to have a wonderful ability to put you at your ease. David insisted that I call him by his first name, and stated I was not to address him in anyway as 'Sir', or 'Your Royal Highness'. David explained, "I had enough of that whilst on earth, like everyone else I am human, and now wish to be addressed in an informal way."

"Ok", I said, "What would you like to tell me then David?"

David smiled pleasantly then said, "Well, where does one start? There is so much to tell you, but some of which will be for another time. Let's start off with where Winston concluded."

I sat waiting for David to speak, before I knew it, a very interesting story was being told to me.

David spoke, "Just after the end of the war, Wallace and I moved to France. As is well known, things were not as easy between myself and others of the Royal Family. As the 'ex' monarch, my presence in England was pretty much unacceptable, but living abroad gave my brother a much better opportunity to rule without about any possible interference. Truth was, and is, that I loved my brother deeply, and would never do anything to harm him or his beloved family."

David paused then continued "However others felt I was somehow a risk to the monarchy and more importantly the establishment within Britain."

"In 1945 Wallace and I returned to France, and more or less lived in peace until 1952."

David continued, "Of course in early 1952 my brother was in the terminal stages of his cancer, and passed away in the February. I had no idea I was considered a threat to the monarchy by some of this group that Winston spoke of earlier. A plan was launched with the purpose of Wallace and I passing in a car accident, thereby negating the possible threat to my niece."

My head was once again whirling; an attempt on David and Wallace's lives was just an incredible concept.

Investigation was required, "Please tell me in what way this attempt was to be made?"

David replied, "A brake failure on the car, causing us to skid off the road and killing us, that was the plan."

"What happened? I mean it obviously failed or was halted, so which way was it?"

David smiled, "Well the plan was put into action, but they failed."

"What happened?"

"Well the brake line was loosened on the car we were about to go out in, but as luck would have it we changed our plans at the last minute and went off in a friend's car instead. When we returned we noticed a pool of fluid, so we had someone come to have a look. Our man took one look and said that without doubt the brake line had been tampered with, had we gone out in the car, our brakes would have failed."

Curiosity stirred and I just had to ask, "Was that the only attempt on your life by this group?"

"Yes," came the reply "Following the coronation I was obviously considered no more of a threat, than had been thought to be the case when my brother was King."

"David, One last question if I may?"

"Of course," David responded.

"As you had abdicated and renounced your right to the throne, why did this group think you were any kind of a threat?" I asked.

"Despite all that happened with my marriage to Wallace, I was still held in high esteem by many within Britain. There were calls for my right to return to the throne to be considered. I denounced such calls, however, there were those who thought I could once again be a problem to the establishment, and hence they 'marked my card' as it were," responded David.
I thanked David for our conversations to date, and asked if I needed to talk to him again would he be willing to do so? He was most agreeable to this and we parted ways with a cheery farewell to each other.

4 DODI AL FAYED

It was a day or so before I could sit again with Spirit. However, things had taken a remarkable change for the better. I was sitting with my dearest companion Susan and under Spirit guidance we sat together, the aim being that I would be entranced by Spirit, and Susan would faithfully record all that was said. It turned out in this first instance to be more awkward than was necessary, this is because all was recorded in longhand, however, Susan did a remarkable job in both recording what was said and in holding a conversation that was revelatory, astounding and in spite of all that she maintained a faithful record as requested by our Spirit friends. Interestingly it wasn't Jimmy Jones who introduced Dodi Al Fayed, but my own guide Chin Lee who spoke first. Gently introduced Susan to the late boyfriend of Princess Diana. What was revealed in that first conversation is reported below:

Chin lee was the first to speak through John in trance, he introduced Dodi to me and told me that he (Dodi) would manifest again for others through John's mediumship.

Dodi commenced our conversation with the words "I was a ladies' man, I flitted like a butterfly, not settling for one until I met Diana. We had such fun together, she really was a light that lit up the whole world."

Dodi paused, and then said to me, "When you speak to my father he will say I was a talkative person, but I have met my match in you."

I laughingly replied, "My job is communication too!"

Our conversation continued, "As I said, I was a ladies' man as people would say, that was my reputation, but Diana was very special to me. In the weeks leading up to our passing, we were very aware that we were being watched and observed, even our driver was aware on occasions that we were being followed."

"You must have been very frightened," I interceded.

Dodi responded, "Well as persons of note within society, it is just part of the package. Of course it was very easy to assume that it was just the paparazzi, but they were not shy in coming forward, and would push a camera in your face and push the button."

"It was more of a concern when we realised that we were being followed, the others didn't rush up to us, they stayed behind us or ahead of us. It was obvious that our telephone conversations were being monitored and I say that because those who were ahead of us must have heard our conversations. Those ahead must have had knowledge of where we were going and how we were going to get there."

A few moments silence passed and then Dodi spoke again. "I was well educated as you can hear. Many people will be wondering whether it was the British Secret Service, and in a way it is both correct and incorrect. There was no direction given from the British Intelligence services for the two of us to be taken out.

"However there were elements within the British Secret Service who had connections with this group that was spoken about by Winston and David. It was this group that were involved in arranging our accident."

I replied, "Your father is angry, and knows it was no accident."

Speaking of his father, Dodi said, "I have spent much time getting into his aura and impressing his thinking, with what I know to be true. He knows that the truth has not yet come out."

Continuing he spoke further "I need to clarify a couple of things that were never really understood, such as why it was that our driver had a large amount of money in his bank account. That money did not come from Diana or myself, nor did it come from the royal family, or the British Intelligence services, but was supplied by this unnamed group, for titbits of information regarding Diana's and my expeditions.

The story continued, "In reality, it was a brilliantly conceived plan, although vicious in its implementation. Members of the paparazzi had been tipped off by the secret group, and were unknowingly drawn into the plot for our demise. What occurred in the tunnel does indeed involve the second vehicle which has never been traced. The second vehicle pulled up level beside us as we were travelling at speed through the tunnel. Just as they edged slightly ahead of us, they used a massive light, like a big lamp, that flashed directly into the front of our vehicle. It was the intensity of the flash that instantly blinded us. That was all that was required, that combined with the alcohol that the driver had been plied with were the ingredient for our fatal 'accident'.

Stunning though this revelation was Dodi continued as if anxious to make sure all the correct information was recorded. "A very clever plan, when you consider that there was no deliberate act of sabotage on the vehicle itself, and the very clean escape of the perpetrators has meant that the only conclusion that could be reached by those investigating would be to record the event as an accident. But it was nothing but cold, calculated murder and the reason behind it, of which there is physical evidence, was their very real concern that the future King Mother was about to become married to a Muslim. Very carefully much of the evidence that would show clearly our intent at the time to become engaged has been carefully removed, including witnesses to the same. The pressures of our place in society were pretty incredible and it is such a shame that two people who loved each other, despite their position in society, should be killed simply because some say they may be considered a threat!

"One other thing I wish to be clear on is that it was not the royal family that requested our removal and it upsets us both that these members have been implicated this way. It is far more connected to the establishment than in any way to the royal family. The one thing this group hadn't taken into consideration is that the dead can speak from beyond the grave!

"I wish to make clear that this is the story I wish to tell. I think it is very important that those throughout the world understand the mechanisations that take place to uphold the power bases of the establishment."

I interjected with "You say that in a powerful way."

Dodi responded gently with "It is a fundamental fact that in the establishment of many countries, and when I say establishment, I refer to the bureaucrats rather than the politicians, for the politicians come and go, but it is the civil servants that try to cling to power."

This initial interview concluded with a final comment meant for Princes William and Harry, from Dodi who said, "I loved Diana very much, and would never have done anything to harm them in any way, but I could not deny the love I had for the woman I adored."

At this juncture it became clear that the energy was dissipating and that Dodi would have to withdraw. When John awoke and we jointly reviewed what had been said, we agreed that if it was possible we would talk to Dodi again, only this time using tape recorders to ensure we got the words from all sides involved down as accurately as possible.

Our wait was not a very long one, the following evening with tape recorder in hand we again sat to allow spirit to talk through John, we were hopeful of course that our request to speak to Dodi again would be agreed to, we were not to be disappointed. What follows is the edited version of the taped conversation, the entire words spoken by Dodi are recorded here, it is merely personal conversation and incidental comments on my part that have been edited out.

Our second sitting began with Chin Lee speaking to me about some personal matters, and then Dodi was once again introduced to continue our conversation.

Dodi commenced with the following. "Well, well, this is interesting to come and talk again, it's very awkward in a way to talk from the Spirit world, not because communication is difficult, but it's this coming close to the physical plane that really dulls the senses. It's a bit foggy, a little bit, well, funny for us and takes a little bit of getting used to. I wanted to carry on a little bit from what I said to you the other day, my beautiful lady."

I interrupted to apologise for not doing much of the writing as we had been busy with other things, Dodi responded by saying "You have recorded all that we have said so far, what more can we ask of you?"

"Well we have this tape recorder now so we should be much more accurate," I said.

"Well let's see what we can come out with then shall we?" replied Dodi, and then continued by saying "I was talking to you and I told you about the, er, light in the tunnel where we were blinded by the 'lamp' as I termed it, and I, something I left out which is equally important, you know I was pretty much out of my body as soon as the impact had occurred, and even though Diana lived very briefly in effect she was also out of the body and so she was not in any pain as such, and I think that is a concern for people here, and especially, and obviously our concern is for the two young men erm, William and Harry, because that must play on their minds er, we both wish to reassure them that there was in, er, as nice as you can make something of such a horrible incident, er I hope that will be of some comfort to them, that we did not suffer."

I tried to give my support to that comment by saying, "I am sure they will be."

Dodi spoke further "Ok erm, I'm not sure what else I need to say to you as well really…"

Dodi paused and remembering a point John had raised I said to Dodi, "I think John erm, when I told John about it, he said that it's all very well saying those things and he understands that, but he says he needs real evidence you know? Evidence that you are speaking about the situation, and evidence that the things that you are telling are things that nobody else knows."

Instantly the response came, "Yes, obviously that is a very good point, er well let me give you a couple of pieces of information, that are not known in the public domain. I had a very heated discussion with my father, just a few days before the incident, of course that has never been made public, er but that is just personal information between him and me, let me think of other things that I can tell that can be verified…"

I commented, "The fact that you've said that, is that your father will say 'yes we did' and er I can imagine he felt quite bad about that when he found out you had 'died'."

"My ring that I was er used to wear on my right hand disappeared and it has been of concern to my father that this has not been recorded anywhere. Er, as far as everyone is concerned, er, they believe I wasn't wearing it at the time, but how did this ring mysteriously disappear?" he said.

"What did the ring look like Dodi?" I asked, curiosity stirred.

"A gold ring, and it was er, how do I say?" said Dodi obviously trying to think of the best way to describe his ring.

"Did it have jewels in it or engraving?" I said trying to be of help.

"It had engraving, of erm, like a coat of arms, a sort of coat of arms."

"Was that from a family, or a family kind of emblem?" I queried.

"Yes, it's connected to the family, it's almost a symbol of the family name, the history, but that ring disappeared and has never been found," stated Dodi.

"Where is it?" I asked.
"It is locked away in a file, it is being kept in a sealed plastic bag and held on file."

" In the police department?"

"No, it is not within the usual…"

"Investigation kind of situation?"

"Yes, it's held by others."

"Who are these others Dodi?"

"The same ones responsible for our passing."

"Why would they want your ring though?"

"Ask them, not me, but them."

Dodi then momentarily paused and continued with further evidence of his survival, "I am trying to rack my brains for other pieces of information that are not publicly known. My father still has many of my personal items, and still has not had them removed, and there are certain areas where everything has been left just as it was, and he still leaves it almost as a shrine to me. I guess in a way that's not particularly evidential, because there will be lots of people who will say don't a lot of parents do that for their children? So let us think of other things here, when I was a child erm, very young, I think I was about eight or nine at the time, well I had a fall out with my father as all children do, and I told my father I was going to run away from home, and I disappeared for several hours, he did get quite concerned about that, but that is also evidence that he can also confirm for you as well.

"He is also very er, you know as I say, I try and get into his energy field, his aura quite often, he is very erm suffering a lot from stress at the moment. He is very distressed at the outcome that was published a week or so ago (referring to the official verdict of UK investigation by Lord Stevens of Kirkwhelpington on December 2006) this is causing him quite a great bit of concern, so I just wish him to know that I understand, but this will help him greatly with what we are speaking about now."

" Is there anyway Dodi, that we could get in contact with him and talk to him, or is it too soon?" I queried.

"The contact that you will have with my father will not be instigated from your end, but it will be coming from a source close to my father, but you will eventually be put in touch with each other. At that point we will be able to erm, pass on some more information, but I think it's probably better if I talk direct to my father. I know that the information that I have already given you should be enough to stir his interest, and warrant a meeting, and with my father you certainly always have to stir his interest enough to guarantee a meeting with him, he is a very busy man, and very discerning, er, but he knows when he hears something that is truth, he will want to speak to me again and I would like the opportunity to speak to him if that's at all possible.

"So I have told you er, several other things, I guess in some ways I guess it's a little bit irrelevant to talk about what has been going on in spirit after we have passed on…"

"Oh no," I said, "It's really interesting.

"Well, er yes but it doesn't really prove an awful lot."

"I know, but I want to know," I said

"Ok, well what have I done," said Dodi thoughtfully.

"What actually happens, when you pass do you go to a place of healing, how does it work?" I asked.

"It does depend on the people involved, and the circumstances of their passing, but for myself and for Diana, we were momentarily aware that we were involved in a car crash, and then of course you lose consciousness. Well my journey was leaving the er shall I say I was aware of voices around, but in the distance as if everyone was drifting away from me, but obviously I was drifting away from them. I became aware of this beautiful white light which immediately drew my attention to it, because it wasn't just because it was a bright light, but it was the love that I could feel from that light and naturally it drew me towards it, but when I actually as I say, I don't know if this is the right word to use, but 'woke' up I was in what you would call a hospital bed for all intents and purposes. That was really not necessary in terms of repairing, or in terms of how you would understand it on earth, because people go in to a hospital because they need medication, surgery or something like that. It is because the conscious mind would expect to find itself in that sort of situation, and it's a way of helping those who have passed in tragic circumstances to come to terms in a more easier way and so the hospitals as such are not necessary in terms of repairing someone's health, but they are necessary in terms of helping people understand what has happened to them, and to help introduce others in the spirit world who will help them adjust to their new life. So I woke up in a hospital bed amazingly feeling absolutely fine, which was really rather odd when you think that you've been in a major accident, but I was fine, and there were nurses and doctors around as you would know them. Obviously as such they were not dispensing tablets or anything but it just was very reassuring in the circumstances. Then I was introduced to er members of the family who had passed over before me, and that was really quite an amazing experience, I have to say that before they were introduced to me, one of the nurses very kindly explained to me that I had passed on, and that I was considered by the earthly world to be 'dead'."

"What was your sense with that? Did you realise you had passed on?" I queried.

"Well I'd realised I'd had an accident of course, and obviously when you wake up, you realise that you are still alive, but what you don't realise instantly is that what is actually happening is that the spirit has left the body, and it is the spirit that is living on. So sometimes it is a little bit of an adjustment that needs to take place with people and it was true in my case as well, I realised quite quickly because there were certain aspects that were really clear. The body was much lighter although I looked at my hands and my body was as I would have recognised it on the earth plane, but I felt lighter, like I was floating, like everything was so much easier, it's very hard to describe in words, but it was quite different, and at first you just think well maybe I must have been on some medication which was making me feel that way, but it was not."

Curious about Diana I asked, "Was Diana with you or did she go to a different area?"

"Diana was in a different room, we were not instantly together, erm but well I won't talk about what her experience was, because I think it would be interesting for you to talk to her and see what happened. We did meet up, and we discussed what had happened."

"What I have read about is that on the spirit level there is that complete unconditional love and I know you had that anyway on the earth, so is it a different feeling when you pass over?" I queried.

"It is in the respect that it is far more intense."
"Really? More intense? Gosh!"

"Yes, your limitation of the physical body dulls the real feeling and senses of the spiritual one, so no matter how intense you may experience love, or unconditional love here, it is like taking a massive leap on to a different level of sensing and feeling and awareness. It is really incredible and so hard to put into words."

I then mentioned the feelings I experience as a medium when my workers are in my aura and the way I experience the unconditional love when they surround me with and I asked Dodi if it was anything like that, his response was "Well I guess it would be hard to imagine it doubled but imagine that magnified fifty times and you might just be getting close to the difference which is very, very intense."

"Were you and Diana part of a 'soul group'?" I asked.

"Well my understanding of it is that I am still an individual, and Diana still operates as an individual," he responded.

"You have got your spirit journey and what you need to learn," I stated hoping to get an insight as to whether Diana and Dodi were connected on a soul level.

Dodi stated, "It is one I am still learning as well, you know people think that you pass to spirit and you suddenly become aware of everything and know everything, and it really isn't quite like that, you understand certain things i.e. that the spirit lives on after death, but if you have an understanding of one way of thinking then you can continue that way of thinking, no-one is actually going to stop you. Even whether that is right or wrong. It is still open for you to find your own pathway. So there are people here living in the spirit world who still follow very passionately their religious way of life, or the sort of clothing they might have worn, and they do that until there is a time that will come to all where the mind says 'this is no longer necessary', so then they move on and things change, but there are still people who live in groups like that.

"Ok, is it like a big garden? Is it towns or villages?" I asked in my innocence.

"It is everything, anything you can think of can exist in the Spirit world. It does not need to exist but it can," replied Dodi.

"So it's almost like manifestation, you just kind of think something and it can be?"

"Sort of, but not quite, for instance people tend to live in houses just as they would on earth, and the houses are solid as you would recognise your building which appears solid to you. Of course our different vibration allows for differing building materials to be used, which are to us are as solid as your bricks and mortar are to you.

"So there are buildings that people can live in, you can find yourself in what you might term sort of city type environments where there are lot of people in a very small space, and others that prefer to live in more rural type locations or even in a certain amount of isolation, because that is what they choose to do, there are so many options open for everybody."

"Dodi, how long, I know time is irrelevant in the Spirit world, but how long roughly would a Spirit wait before they decide to possibly come back again?"

"Well, from where I am, I have not seen anyone who has come back, so I don't know how to answer that. Everybody that I have met here, there has been one, no there were two, that we call them 'moved on' but they haven't come back as I know it to the earth, they've moved on to different realms within the Spirit world. A sort of passing, but it's not the same, it's as if you erm, try the best analogy I can give you is a fish that lives in the sea that doesn't know that above the sea there is land that you could walk on. It is like the fish being able to suddenly discover that it has a different set of lungs and can walk, and can gravitate to this new area, it's all part of the same, just its understanding has changed that allows it to move into a different vibration of energy, which effectively what is the change is there."

I then said to Dodi "I can understand that maybe John and I contracted somehow is before incarnating to come together to be part of this project and to share part of this life together. In the case of you and Diana was that also part of a pre-agreed contract, including maybe the way you passed together?"

The response was swift "No matter how difficult this is for some people to understand, it was something that unfortunately did have to happen. It had to happen so that people could also understand what is going on in their governments, and not just their governments, but behind the scenes of governments, and how power is abused, and how people are being really fed propaganda, that tells them things are okay, when actually there is a lot of underhanded work going on behind the scenes. So in that respect, yes it was contracted out because it was needed, and although that is a painful thing for some to come to terms with, because of their understanding is very much based on the physical plane of existence, it will be hard for them to understand that people may have been involved in something which ultimately meant their lives would cease on the earthly level, but would actually have a greater impact on the earthly plane."

Agreeing with Dodi I said, "I believe that, because of things like the 'twin towers', and things like foot and mouth disease, all those sorts of things, I think they are all things for people to realise what they are doing, the impact their thoughts have, and their decisions and directions have."

Dodi then commented, "Quite right, and I have learnt so much since I came here because I came to the Spirit World really not knowing anything about it in all honesty, well only what Diana had told me, you know I was very much a cynic and material as well. What I could see and touch was what I knew existed. So it was a little bit difficult but I knew that Diana felt so passionately about it that I obviously did pay attention to what she said, but even so, to find yourself in this environment was quite an amazing revelation. I then embarked on this journey of discovery and questioning which is why I am able to answer some of what you have asked me. There are things that I know that you may ask, that I can't possibly answer, but I would probably be able to ask the gentleman Chin Lee, because he has a great deal of knowledge so he has been very helpful as have others here, so that's been very interesting, but I'm still on that journey of discovery."

"Gosh, that's really lovely to hear actually, that you don't instantly know everything, that it is a continuing journey," I said.

"People talk of having your life flash before your eyes," said Dodi, "that really does happen when you pass, you have an opportunity to review all that you have experienced in your life, from the very earliest moment of your arrival in absolute finite detail."

"Is that the Akashic records?" I queried.

"Well, yes, yes that is what they would be called the, Akashic records. Everything that has ever happened recorded, there is nothing that anybody does in their life that can be avoided. You can pretend on the earth plane 'that you did this or you didn't do that', it is recorded it is an unavoidable thing that you will have to face at some point," commented Dodi.

Feeling very aware of my own transgressions I said, "I have done some naughty things in the past."

"No, I don't think you have done as many bad things as you think," said Dodi.

He continued, "I do not think you will have much to worry about, the great many good things you have done, far outweigh any of the minor misdemeanours you speak of."

For a moment Dodi loses his focus and I knew the session was about to end, however, he shortly returns and says, "Just for a moment there I lost my focus and it pulled me out of the energy. I heard what you said, and yes I do think it is appropriate for me to withdraw now. I think I've given you all I can for now. If you need to call me, obviously I will do my very best to be available because I think this work you are both involved in is very important.

"Keep writing down all that you are given, and others will add more to what has been said. You will also be in touch, as I am being led to understand here, with others still living on your earth plane, who will become involved as well," added Dodi.

"In what way? What do you mean?" I asked.

"In providing information, so you will have, if you like, evidence from those of us who have passed on, and also evidence from those living on the earth plane."

"But it will come?" I asked concerned that maybe people may not be interested.

Dodi laughed and said, "You do not think that so many of us have come, and put in all this effort, for it just to be put on one side?" came the response.

"I think the thing is when we are on the earth plane, and our lives have been simple. For John and I, it's hard to believe that will happen," I commented.

At this point Dodi needed to withdraw, and our conversation with him was at an end for now. We couldn't wait on hearing the tape at the end of the session as to who would come and talk to us next; we were not to be disappointed.

5 PRINCESS DIANA

Our introduction to Princess Diana came via Chin Lee, the principal control of John. He spoke to me briefly about some personal issues and then very calmly introduced Diana to me, after explaining how difficult it would be for Diana to communicate through the vocal chords of a man. Chin Lee then stepped back leaving the way clear for Diana to speak to me through John.

As Diana stepped into John's energy and tried to communicate it was an obvious struggle at first as she needed to get used to being in close contact with the earth plane and the processes required to make communication successful. I explained to her in the following way.

"This will be strange, because this is a man's energy," I said.

Using John, Diana nodded and indicated she understood.

Diana's first clear words were "It's an odd feeling."

Not hearing clearly as the words were mumbled and difficult at first, I asked, "A lot of feeling?"

"An odd feeling to feel so aware of your physical world," she replied, her command of the voice becoming much stronger than at first. Diana continued, "And to try and be aware of a physical body."

"Does it remind you of how it was?" I asked.

Diana responded, "I'd forgotten how dense, and how sluggish is the physical world is, and I had never thought on the earth plane of that, and yet now, I realise how sluggish the physical body was. It is very strange to talk through a man's voice, so different, I can work with this, it is ok, it's just I am trying to get to grips with this, and it is really quite interesting. You are a very gentle soul, it is nice that we have the opportunity to speak, and although it is a little bit unusual if you like, talking through a man, it is very pleasant as I am able to talk to a woman, who will understand the sensitivities of being, and how society judges a woman so much by her actions, where a man can perform many actions and be praised for, what a woman would be condemned for."

"I think that's been the way for a very, very long time, and it still continues," I replied.

"It's not fair, <pause> anyway, you have much you wish to ask I know," said Diana.

"Shall we talk first of the incident?" inquired the Princess.

"Yes!" I replied.

"What would you like to know?" asked Diana.

"Dodi, very kindly spoke about the situation and your relationship, without going into detail, because he wanted you to talk to me about the aspects of the relationship that I asked. He told me much of his own experiences, and that you lived shortly after the accident where he had passed instantly," I replied.

"This is very true, that my physical body was continuing to exist after that of Dodi, but you know people assume that because the physical body is still in operation, that therefore the spirit must still be within it, and it is not necessarily true. The spirit body, as mine was, can still be attached to the physical body but not be within it as such, and I was thrust out of my body but it wasn't immediately detached, whereas Dodi was, his passing was immediate, mine was a short time afterwards."

"What's the feeling that goes with that Diana?"

"It is very odd, in a very strange way, because you would expect to be very aware of the physical injuries sustained but in fact you are not. The Spirit is basically thrust out of the body, so physical pain is totally missing, and there is just this feeling of peace and serenity as you prepare to really engage into your new-found life within the spiritual realms. So it is not really as traumatic a picture as is painted, it is far more serene than those that would make films or dramas would have you believe, but the reality is that it is a far more peaceful process."

"Is it more that you ease into it?"

"I think that is probably an easier way of saying it too, because it is not something you immediately adjust to, very few people, even those that are sensitive are not always easily able to adjust, some people do and some people don't. The vast majority I think are very much like Dodi and I where our adjustment was fairly quick, but not instantaneous."

"I think Dodi really appreciates the understanding and thoughts you had about the spirit world and understanding about life after life. I think he really appreciates the fact that you talked about that."

"He was of course very sceptical," commented Diana. Continuing, Diana said, "It was wonderful that I could plant a seed in his thought so that when the time came it really wasn't a complete and utter shock for him as it might have been. I was so grateful to all those mediums and psychics I had to come into contact with because they had helped me be more aware of what happens at the point of what we call death. Indeed all that knowledge helped me when I was trying to help those on the earth deal with their terminal illnesses and things like that, I could cope with it far more easily knowing that they would be going to a bright and beautiful place."

I addressed Diana's relationship with Dodi and said, "Dodi talked about your relationship in a very respectful way, and a loving way without telling me about how you felt and what happened to you at that point and what your plans were to be together."

"It was very difficult, we felt very strongly about each other, and we had great plans at the time we were forced out of our bodies."

"What plans did you have?"

"Dodi had asked me to marry him, and we were in the process of setting things up for that to be announced, and really we think now having discussed it since passing that really somebody did think of us a threat, which is why we were dispensed with."

"Were you thinking of having more children?" I asked, curious to know what plans she and Dodi had.

"We had not really gone into very deep discussion about that, but it was a subject that had been muted but we had no firm decision for that."

"You weren't pregnant?"

"That was something that was planned for the future," came the reply.

I pushed further and asked, "You weren't pregnant at that point?"

"I don't wish to discuss it, I don't think it will help anybody, I think a rather more important thing is that there were those who did consider a joining together of myself and Dodi would be very detrimental to the monarchy, or should I say more importantly, to the establishment within the United Kingdom. I don't bear any grudges against members of the royal family. I think unfortunately they are also pawns in the games of the establishment, and it has been very easy for the establishment to allow, and maybe even encourage claims, that somehow the royal family were involved in our demise, when it clearly was not the case. I think for my two sons, who I love dearly, it is very important that they know that."

We then chatted for a while about her two sons William and Harry. Diana expressed the opinion that both of them are naturally shy, although acknowledged that Harry is far more outgoing than his brother. When I asked if there was anything John and I could give her sons in the future she said, "They are both very sensitive young men, and in many ways I am able to influence their thinking. So in a way I would have to say there is not anything that you would need to say or do, because they are certainly on a soul level as we call it, a soul level, aware of my influence round and about them. I am really very deeply proud of them both."

Speaking of William, Diana expressed the following: "William is doing very, very well. He will make a very great King one day. Although I can't be with him in the physical sense, I will do my utmost to guide him for the best path for his people that he is here to reign over, so I shall do my best to help and guide him. Equally I shall do my best to influence Harry and I will give him as much love and help that I can from my new perspective within the Spirit world."

"Diana, is there anything else that you can tell us that anybody else wouldn't know, because the problem we have obviously writing this book and giving evidence about yours and Dodi's story in a sensitive way, we have to give evidence that other people wouldn't have known in the public arena, do you understand our concern?" I asked.

Diana softly began to sing a nursery rhyme "*Hush little baby, don't you cry, momma's gonna sing you a lullaby.*"

I asked if she sang this rhyme to both boys? to which she nodded affirmatively.

When asked if she had anything else she would like to say, Diana responded with. "There are things I would love to say, some would not be appropriate I suppose for someone of my considered opinion."

Having got a bit confused as to what Diana was referring to, she clarified what she wanted to talk about by saying, "I am not talking about what I would like to say to my children, there are some people that I would like to say other comments to, but it would be most inappropriate to do so, given my past position."

When I asked her what relevance her past position had now, she responded by saying, "It does not matter for me, but it does matter for my children, and for their sakes I don't think it's appropriate for me to rock the boat too much."

"Would you like to comment about the royal family?"

Diana spoke again softly, "Shall we say not so much the Royal Family, but some that supposedly were there to serve and support. I feel very let down. One who swore he would defend me and support me, come what may…"

"Charles?" I proffered.

"No, not Charles, Paul," corrected Diana.

"What was his surname?"

"Paul Burrell, but he was at one point a very good friend."

"Was he ever anything more than that? He has been heard to suggest that your relationship was more than just good friends."

"No, that is just his wild fantasy! He abused our friendship, and I am very disappointed in how he has conducted things since I passed on, but that is something for him to deal with," said Diana. Still speaking softly she continued. "It is a disappointment, not so much about what people say or don't say about me, I'm not here to listen to it any more, but I do worry obviously about my two young sons, and that is my concern, is what these comments may do to them in terms of impact and affecting their daily lives."

We then discussed several matters some personal on both sides of life. I pointed out to Diana that both her sons would have chosen their earthly life before incarnating, and that therefore I felt that they would be strong enough to withstand any of the negativity that may impact on their lives.

In our conversation we discussed the difficulties many people have in dealing with financial limitations that seemed not to apply so much in a person's life which seemed to be one of privilege. Diana as always responded in a pleasant manner saying, "A lot of people will think that my life was just one of privilege, I did have an understanding of financial matters, even more so following my divorce really. It really brings things home to you when suddenly resources that were open to you are withdrawn."

Diana then became aware that she would have to withdraw as the conditions were no longer appropriate, but before she left, she promised to return again so we could chat some more. I could hardly wait!

6 JIMMY AND DIANA

Following our usual greetings with Chin Lee, we were once again led into a fascinating session, with a further opportunity to talk to both Jimmy Jones, and Diana, Princess of Wales.
Chin Lee introduced Jimmy as our first communicator of the evening.

"Hello!" came the cheery sound of a young man with an East London accent.

"It's nice to meet you," I said. "I've heard lots about you."

"My name's Jimmy, Jimmy is me name. I was 22 but you know that. It's funny cos you're holding my hand, I never had a girlfriend. There was a girl I liked, but it was never more than eyes, our eyes would make contact, I never knew a girl."
Jimmy continued, "This is a bit weird coming here, there's all sorts of things here not there."

"What do you mean, all sorts of things?"

"For us it's hard to come here, it's like you're going through a dark tunnel and then you come back in contact with one of these bodies and cor is it heavy, it's like er that expression when you say 'like walking through treacle'. Well it's like that, walking through thick treacle."

"Have you done it quite often?"

"Well I've not spoken like this, but I've got close before cos I was speaking to John. Well that was difficult enough but this is erm, well I don't think I am doing too bad?"

"You're doing brilliantly!"

"You have to really focus, on the body, keeping it breathing and operating the throat and all that. It's really odd, but it's okay. Anyway, you know I was killed in World War One?"

"Yes."

"You know I was with the Lancashire Regiment?"

"No I didn't know that until John told me."

"You can tell by my accent I wasn't from around Lancashire. My dad was, but I spent a lot of time around, you know, er, you get together as youngsters; I was 22, well a bit younger than that when we joined up. Of course a lot of our boys, we all met up, different boys from different places, I had a lot of mates from down London way and you can't help but pick up their accent. Not like the Lancashire accent. I never really had one until I got in the army. Interesting accent, anyway what can I tell you?"

"How did you die?"

"Well I was er, just being ordered over the top, just like everybody else, but what happened was, you sort of had like er, forget what the right word is for them now, but we were put in like little groups and in each little group you had your own engineer come soldier type guy whose job was to deal with any logistic problems as well as they'd have a rifle and do all that as well. He got shot, silly bugger, yeah, he got machine gunned he was trying to put one of them duck boards down over this barbed wire and of course Jerry saw him coming and he copped for it. He hadn't laid the board across so we still had the problem. So there we was in our little trench, ordered to go out, but we weren't going to go out just to get mown down, so who's going to go up and do the duckboard? We hurriedly picked straws and I got the short straw. So I get up there, luckily though I did get me duckboard across, but I never got to cross it. I don't really remember feeling anything, I don't really remember any pain either."

"Did you get shot?"

"Yeah, all I remember was, I knew I must have been hit, but I was like dead before I hit the ground."

"Well that's good that you didn't really have any pain?"

"Yeah, but when you are 22 and you want to go and fight for your King and country you don't sort of contemplate ending like that. You've all got these ideas of being like er the old British soldier who charges in with all guns blazing, and maybe going in shining glory. Of course for most of us that never happened we were just gunned down in our thousands, stupid bastards. Stupid they were ordering us out like that, didn't achieve really nothing. They just kept on killing, kept on killing, slaughtering, horrible!"

"Jimmy, was it the First World War where many soldiers said they saw angels?"

"It was yeah, many of the guys saw these images, have to say I wasn't one of them, but I did hear stories, and I spoke to people who were taken over as I was, and they all saw that as a sign that we shouldn't really be fighting each other. But you just do as you are ordered, if you didn't you was taken out and shot anyway. Either way you was going to have it weren't ya? They were going to shoot you if you went over the top, and or if you didn't, you was a coward so they shot you anyway."

"Would you have liked to have been born in this time?"

"I was born when I was meant to be born, I chose to come back and live that life and pass in that way, but of course at the time you just think here I am not really having done anything, and I think many of us were resentful when we got to Spirit cos it was like we'd died for King and country, and what was the reward really?"

"Was your name recorded?"

"Oh yeah, it's down there, my name's only really interesting in respect of what it means later on in this book, it's relevant to the whole story. Me as an individual, no, I am just lucky to have been invited to participate and it's been great fun. I mean you know we'd never met…course we'd heard of Churchill, cos he was war minister you know in the first war. Not until much later did he become really famous, he was just another politician at that time and he took a right bashing cos he'd cocked it all up hadn't he? To meet him in person here, and to be involved in this story has been really interesting."

"Can you see the environment you are in now?"

"To be honest, I can't, it's very dark here. I mean it's the density of your condition really, but I can hear you really clear, and I don't think I'm having too much of a problem talking to you. Chin Lee, he's a funny bloke he is, he's been really helpful and he's shown me what to do and in a way I guess you'd say I've been practising, just not speaking. This is really lovely to talk to you, first girl I've spoken to in years! Let's talk about this story then shall we, you know about Winston coming through, and what he said, and I know you read about David, the Duke of Windsor."

"And Dodi and Diana," I interjected.

"Yes, them two as well. The story continues there is more information I know Diana wishes to share with you. I do apologise that I wasn't able to come and speak to you earlier, I would have liked to have done that before Diana came to speak to you, but we didn't really have the time then to do that and it was quicker and more efficient for Chin Lee to do that. Tonight I wanted the opportunity just to come and say hello. Can you see me?"

"I can only really see John's face right now."

"No, no, I'm sorry I didn't really explain myself there. When I say 'see me' I don't mean see me as in seeing me with your eyes. I mean clairvoyantly."

" Oh, let me see, <brief pause> are you raising your hat? I can see you now, winking at me, you are a cheeky boy!"

"Mind you I stunk a bit."

"Stunk? I can't smell that though!"

"Cos you know, when you are in them trenches you can't just nip out and have a bath!"

"I feel you had a heart of gold you know?"

"Well I really believed in what we were fighting for, and I believed we did it all for the very right reasons you know. You can't just march into someone's country and just take it over! That's got to be stopped hasn't it? So we did what we thought was right at the time. You can moan about it but it was still an experience that I wouldn't have been without. Sometimes you wouldn't get food for a couple of days, and then you'd find there was terrible rain, a quagmire, and your boots would fill up and then you could never get your feet dry, and so if you didn't get shot you were just as likely to die of foot rot."

"There were other diseases weren't there?"

"You imagine what it was like, thousands of people being slaughtered, rain water everywhere, blood running into the rain water, bodies left for days, weeks on end cos you couldn't go and recover them. The gunfire was constant either them firing at us, or us pounding them in return, and what did we do? We ended up moving a few miles over several months and that was it, and several thousand men dead."

"Can you remember the name of a mate that you had?"

"Mates came and went you know, you didn't try and get too close to no-one cos you'd meet someone one day and think he's a real nice guy and he was dead. One of them was called Jack Barber, what a name eh? He couldn't cut a blinkin hair if he tried!"

"Did you write home to your parents?"

"Well when you could, as I say just trying to get food and ammunition to us sometimes was a nightmare let alone the letters, or even sending them back. You weren't even sure that what you had sent was ever going to be sent back anyway because the communications were very disjointed. In fairness it was just as bad for those on the other side."

"Were your mother and father alive at the time you were fighting?"

"They died after me obviously."

"Have you met up with them?"

"Oh yeah, of course I have, and that was a day to remember that was!"

"Did you greet them?"

"Oh yeah, wouldn't have missed that for the world would I? You imagine the looks on their faces when I was standing there it was like 'Jimmy! Jimmy! My Jimmy!" You should have seen me mother's face! That was a sight for her to realise that she hadn't really lost me forever. That was something special it really was and I'd waited so long for her to understand that."

"Did you try and impress your thoughts onto her once you had passed over?"

"Everyone does that, cos you're alive you want everyone to know, not everyone's able or ready to accept that. Anyway I guess we need to move on with this story, now you was having quite a chat with Diana, I know that cos I was standing around listening, I think like, if my name's involved I ought to know what is going on. Of course I didn't know who this lady was, it might sound odd to you lot, but she was way after us, she's a mere youngster to us. Quite odd really, there was I at the age of 22, but in her life span I'd have been an old man if I had lived that long. Here she was, coming over like that, terrible, terrible."

"It really shocked the nation."

"Well, yeah, you could feel in the spirit world the love that poured out from the earth plane, we realised how strongly she pulled people towards her and, I hate to say it, but some people worshipped her, which I don't think was good, but that was a bit sort of not right, but the love that was felt for her was genuine, and she was, is, I should say is a very genuine lady who does care very deeply about different things you know. I think I'd better shut up really; I'll let her come and talk to you. I just wanted to pop in, and it was just meant to be a brief little chat. Here we are having a good old natter and the poor lady's been standing there waiting for ages to come and speak. I just wanted to apologise for not introducing her to you the other night, so I am trying to make up for it now by taking the opportunity to introduce her on a more formal basis. I'm going to step back and we'll let Diana try and come and talk to you again. See you soon love, nice to talk to you."

With that Jimmy was gone and I waited for Diana to come back and speak to me again.

Diana began, "I spoke before and it was odd then, it is still just odd, as my voice is not as I would like it to be, it really isn't. I would never have been so deep, really rather strange."

"Can you hear it, can you hear the voice?" I asked

"It sort of echoes back at me and it's very much... obviously you can hear it's through a man's vocal chords and that's really rather odd."

"Maybe you can try Diana to come through me one day?"

"That would be very nice, we should do that I think, it would be very nice. You know I have forgotten where we were talking the other day. We talked about quite a few things didn't we?"

"Yes, we talked about the crash, the accident."

"Accident? Huh!"

"Well, the crash, it wasn't an accident, but that's what we've been conditioned to accept and so they are the words that come to mind."

"Do you know there is some more very compelling evidence that is going to come out very shortly, which is also why there is such an urgency for the book, and the words that are being written here? But there are certain people who will be implicated by the evidence that is going to arise. It is not the evidence of us here in Spirit that will generate that evidence, but the evidence is there and has been waiting in a cupboard almost for someone to pull it out.

Well it should be very funny from our side of life to see it and watch as the sparks go flying. It will be very interesting to watch."

"Diana, this information, is it going to come out after our book?"

"Well you might be quite surprised because there is very much a deliberate plan that almost simultaneously is probably the best way to describe it and some will say well did this book come first or this other information? Such is the timing."

At this point Diana seems to have trouble working through John's body and a short break took place. Diana then returned and explained a little of the difficulties involved.

"You have to deal with so many things, of course the real focus is to get the words out, but it's not as easy as just thinking and working the vocal chords, you have to consider all the other actions you have forgotten as you are now in the spirit where problems such as breathing are not an issue, but they are for a physical body so we have to try and bear in mind all the natural operation of the physical body is going through, and that can be quite disconcerting. The slightest movement within the physical body, which you are not expecting can be enough just to throw us out of balance. I mean the body of John, if he has any problems going with the digestion or anything and it affects the body then it affects our connection. Also the outside contacts have an impact as well."

Our connection was once again disturbed by discomfort with John. A brief period passed by, and I was joined again by Chin Lee, John's principal worker.

"Greetings to you child, I am sorry for the interruption. There was again a little bit of imbalance. Just bear with us while we try and make adjustment in the instrument."

Chin Lee explained that the instrument (John) was uncomfortable due to indigestion problems and this was the cause of our break in communication. Once settled, Diana returned once more.

"That was just like when I passed, you sort of ..." At this point communication was broken for a brief period due to the tape running out. After a quick change the conversation continued with Diana completing her sentence as follows.

"... are thrown out as in terms of the mind connection, and I suddenly lost it."

"That was John eating too quickly! I said."

"You remember that I had problems with eating as well? There was a time I really became quite ill actually. It was a time when I was really struggling and it's very true to say that all these things happen because of problems within. I don't mean people being mentally ill, but it is within the mental level of their thinking that does have an impact on to the physical. Really what often happens, not always, but what quite often happens is that the manifestation in the physical body is a direct result of what we are thinking, and what we experience.

"Part of my philosophy is disease in the mind equals disease in the body!"

"True, very true. Anyway following our last conversation, is there anything that has come to mind that you would like to know?"

"One thing I'd really like to know, and I know you said it really wasn't relevant, but I know I asked you if you were carrying a baby at the time? You said it wasn't relevant."

"Well I suppose in some ways it is relevant, as some people feel there is a need to understand a little bit of what was going on so in that respect I suppose I ought to be clear on that. I didn't want to say it because I don't want to cause Harry and William any stress you see."

"Do you want us to not put it in the book?"

"You know, instead of answering directly the question, what I will say is it really doesn't matter what you say or don't say, because there are always those who will make their own mind up, and whether you say well, their death was an act of murder, or whether you say their death was an accident, there will always be those who believe the opposite. It doesn't really matter how much evidence you provide to the contrary, that is what they wish to believe. So in answer to your question, yes, I was carrying a child."

"Did you meet up with the soul of the baby?"

"Yes, yes. But I don't wish to say any more on that, simply because I had to experience so much on the earth plane, I don't want to be drawn into that sort of what does the baby look like, is it a boy or is it a girl. You would not believe the questions that were thrown at you from those awful, awful reporters. A lot of them were not just not very nice people, but they would get close to you, and they would smell, and ugh it was awful. Sometimes they just didn't have any respect, not because I was someone of supposed royal rank, but they just didn't care about people, they were just interested in their story."

"So William and Harry, we read in the newspapers that they feel it was an accident, but I don't feel that they believe that, and that's just my personal opinion, and I think that's just written for writing's sake."

"Of course, a lot of what is issued in the name of Royal members of the Family, is really governed by the royal household, not necessarily even Her Majesty, much more the, as you say, the public relations team."

"What about James Whittaker?"

"Well privately we always used to say he was a royal pain in the a***, but I don't suppose we could print that could we?"

"Well we could, after all they can hardly come and get you!"

"In fairness he was one of the better ones. He did try to present a more unbiased viewpoint, but he did also sometimes try very carefully to please certain people <Diana giggles>. As I say he was one of the better ones, not like the dreadful paparazzi that I have to say I am mortified by this idea that the paparazzi should take complete and utter blame for our deaths because it's so not correct. It's very convenient to pin the blame on people in that field, and although some of them are awful people to blame them for something that was clearly not their fault was completely unfair. I have some interesting news for you as well <giggles> do not tell anyone. William is very in touch, and yes well, shall I say he is incredibly sensitive and he has spoken to me, and he is in contact with me, but it is something that he keeps a little bit quiet."

"Does he know about the book?"

"No, he doesn't know, but he does know that I am up to something. It is very, very difficult because I obviously wish to protect my children, but at the same time I cannot let this matter lie. It's so important, because it's not about really even getting justice for myself or Dodi, it's about helping the people, the general public, understand what is going on in their country, what is sometimes done in their name and not even by the legitimate forces the democratically emplaced authorities, it's those who set themselves up as the un-elected authorities who cause problems and it does bother me immensely the damage it has done to the royal family, because it really is not right to place the blame in that direction. You could blame a lot more things on the royal family, but certainly not that, because it is totally incorrect. I think that's really very important for the general public to be aware that it was nothing that was generated from the royal family itself. That has been of quite a concern, just the implication that it might have been would have an impact on my son and his position and his ability to go forward and rule without that awful thought, I wish to make it clear for his sake. He will be a very good and just King, and he will fight as he does now, for what he knows to be right, and he can be very strong on that you know. Sometimes quite funny, he will tackle his grandmother and, of course she'd probably be quite upset to know that I was there, but of course she can't stop me, but he does stand up to her and I am very proud of him, very proud. He is a lovely young man and he has met a very nice young lady, there will be news this year. It will be very interesting, poor child, hope she knows what she is letting herself in for."

"Are you happy about that?"

"Oh yes, she adores him, it's a real love, that's much more important than one that would chase him for his position, she loves him for who he is, and I can't ask for anything more. No mother can, can they? No mother can."

"Well I haven't been a mother yet, but I can imagine that's how it would be."

"You will, you will! I must go now."

"Okay Diana, well thank you for coming again."

****

Following the announcement on the 14th April 2007 that William and Kate had split, we were aware that this brought into question details as given to us by Diana, as reported above. In an attempt to resolve the discrepancy, we arranged to sit with Spirit on the 15th April 2007 with the hope that Diana would join us and shed some light on the recent revelation. Our conversation is reported as below and is inserted here for obvious reasons:

We greeted each other in our usual way of a simple hello to each other. Diana began by saying:

"I understand from your earthly perspective how all this seems so confusing, yet it is far simpler than people would have you believe. I have been trying for several hours today to step into John's energy, and trying to speak to you. I am very aware of the issue of William and Kate and their decision to split. It is very simple, you understand of course how we can see things from this perspective, but not always can you see clearly exactly what is going to happen in the future. I did not mention what was going to happen other than that there would be an announcement, and I did say that I was quite pleased with that, I would have been happy of course if it made my son happy. But the story is not over yet, it's not over yet."

"Is it a decision to say this just because they wanted a break really from the pressure?" I asked.

"Not exactly, it is a decision they have been guided with. It is a reluctant decision really, but you know isn't it strange how people react? They expect all those in the Spirit world to be somehow totally infallible, to be able to see things exactly as they will be. There is such a lack of understanding about all this."

"Of course, what I said several months ago, as far as I could tell everything was going along smoothly. I will tell you of possibilities that still may be there, but they will be hard to prove because the individual choice of people, their free will as it were, it was very much within their decision making to become engaged, but not at this present moment obviously from what they have said. It was also reported that William was to wed Kate in about four years time. Kate has been under the most awful pressure, absolutely awful."

"They are likening that to you Diana, when you were under so much pressure," I said.

"Of course, the future Queen, is undoubtedly going to come under the same public and media scrutiny as I did, and possibly even more nowadays. So incredible pressures on the young lady, and you know she does still love him passionately."

"Why did they have to make that decision Diana?"

"It is, shall I say, politics really. It is all to do with them both being very aware that William will be very tied up with his military career for another three or four years, which is why he was keen to have the announcement made that they would marry when he was 28. But of course that was not really enough, they were trying to ease the pressure on themselves by making that announcement. But then they came to an understanding that the lifestyle that would have meant, and the difficulties that would have meant for them to meet up would be difficult. The decision is not necessarily a finite one. One of the possibilities is that they will come back together again. But it is almost about giving each of them a little bit of leeway to find themselves and to give themselves a space without being pressurised for the next four years by the paparazzi and media generally. To be pursued into a marriage, which although be a wonderful event, would be one that is created out of pressure and not correct for them to be involved in."

We discussed dealing with people who may have doubts about why Spirit people may be able to be inaccurate with predicting the future. To which Diana commented:

"Being in the Spirit world and being of royal rank does not give me access to some supreme knowledge, I am no different from anybody else, I can see possibilities, but not necessarily definite outcomes as all are subject to free will. So I am as fallible as everybody else, in the respect that I can see something that I perceive may be coming up in the future, and maybe wish that it will be a good thing for my son. But it is all subject to the free will of the people involved."

"The problem for us is that we now have doubts in our minds, and with that in mind we are all finding it hard to move forward," I said.

"Partly the problem here is the lack of understanding, and this is common across the media in general, there is this misconception that those who have passed on are suddenly illuminated and have access to the certain future, and that is not correct, and that is something that people need to be aware of as well. It's completely misguided to believe that we are infallible. We are entitled as we were on the earth plane to have our own wishes and desires, but that doesn't mean that they will turn out that way. We have the same freedoms to wish and express our own opinion even. I am not sure if I have said all that I can to convince you, in some ways it is very easy to explain, but I can see the dilemma that you have. There is this mind set that 'if you are in Spirit, and are someone of that sort of rank that you must be 100% correct', which of course is incorrect."

Later in our conversation Diana stated:

"I do believe that he has met a very lovely young lady in Kate, and they are going through a traumatic time at the moment. As I said there are several possibilities which I can mention, one being that they will get back together, get engaged and get married. Another being that they will stay separated and go their own ways, another being that having gone their own ways they would eventually find someone else. Personally I do not see that at the moment, at the moment I see him very much connected to Kate, but that is how I perceive things at this present moment in time. It could work out in a month's time that my perception is completely wrong. But I am only able to see the possibilities, but it will be down to William and Kate as to whether they come back together again, or really go their separate ways. All I can tell you at the moment is that the love link between them is very much there. There are pressures being placed on these two young people that are not necessarily of their own choosing. Ultimately there is that element of free will that can move a possibility to be much stronger than another. We are open to the same fallibilities as you are on the earth plane, we have slight possibilities of seeing some possibilities in the future, and our own wishes and desires can equally affect our perception of what we see. There are all these possibilities that can come into it, and yet somehow we in the Spirit world are expected to have developed golden wings and a perfect insight into all that could be. We can do our best, we look at the greatest possibilities, but I will say it again to you, this story is not over yet as regards William and Kate."

Diana then advised us she needed to withdraw, and advised us that Chin Lee wanted to speak as well. Promising to come back should we need her help, Diana then left and we were soon speaking once more to Chin Lee.

****

"Good evening Chin Lee."

"Good evening child. As I said, you know this book was never meant to be just telling a story, it is about also making people understand the problems connected with Spirit communication, and what better way for us to show that than through someone so prominent and so much in the forefront of peoples minds as that of the Princess, the young lady. I know it has made things a little bit uncertain, but it is necessary part of it as well. It is also as Diana has said, the story of William and Kate is far from over."

Our original December 2006 session with Diana concluded with some private comments, which were delightful; as Diana withdrew we were briefly joined by Chin Lee.

"Thanks for popping back Chin Lee."

"It takes many year of practice you know, but yes it is getting in some ways easier because we are working so often together, and the more we work the easier it is for me to blend with the mediums energy. Well that was very interesting. <pause> The instrument is struggling, we speak again soon child, I must go as he will not settle so it is best for him to come back, but have lots of fun, and we speak again, and the love of spirit to you both."

Chin Lee withdrew, although the Christmas holidays were almost upon us, we were excited as to what would happen next in this roller coaster story. We were not to be disappointed with what happened next.

7 TERRORISTS AND LANDMINES

Our next sitting took place between Christmas 2006 and New Year 2007, Chin Lee once again commenced proceedings and we were once again joined by Diana. We tried before this sitting to take the opportunity for Diana to possibly talk through Susan, but this proved more difficult for all involved than we had originally thought. Our conversation therefore continued with Diana using the vocal chords of John and I once again asking the questions.

I welcomed Diana and apologised for the fact we were not able to work as we had thought we might be able to, to which she replied "That's okay. It's not as easy as people think is it?"

"No, not at all."

"It is odd speaking through a man's voice, because it is so different from my own. It is getting a little easier each time we do it, so that is good, but it is still odd for me, it is still rather strange."

"I was thinking about you today, because I was looking at wedding dresses and it reminded me of you in your wedding dress."

"Yes, that of course was a very long time ago wasn't it. I think the saying is 'least said soonest mended' isn't it? I think all that happened in connection with my wedding to Charles has been so well reported it is, well it would be a bit odd to just go over the same old ground, but I think everyone is fully aware what took place and how our marriage deteriorated and ended up as we did."

"Were you happy that day though, when you got married?"

"I was both happy and very nervous of course, it's not just marrying the future King it was being aware of all those eyes upon you, and worrying that you would make a mistake…"

"It would be held in history," I interjected.

"Exactly, so all those things were spinning around in my head a little, but actually no, I have to say I did really enjoyed the occasion, it was very memorable but obviously now I look at it with quite different eyes. I think that's only to be expected by anybody who goes through a marriage and you do that, and think that you will be with that person for the rest of your life, you have no idea that maybe things will go wrong and you enter into that spirit of something that is there for life. But of course it is as things unfold that where you have that maybe set idea of those things that your opinions can change and a realisation that maybe just to stay married is not always the best answer.

"That to be free again, to be with someone who loves you for who you truly are is far more important than a marriage of position or anything of the sort. So, yes, I did enjoy the original day, but I view it all a little bit differently now."

"So what else would you like to say Diana about the situation, the crash or anything else you might like to talk about?"

"I think I've sort of given very much a lot of the detail of the crash and what happened, I wonder if it is also worth talking about my immediate experience after leaving the body because I think that might be of interest."

"Dodi talked about that, and said that he would let you talk about your experience."

"Mine was slightly different from Dodi's, because Dodi was sort of, as you say, instantly thrown out of his body and the spiritual cord as I understand it that connects the body to the spirit was immediately severed so his journey was slightly different from mine. I was thrust out of my physical body, but my physical body was able to support life for a short period of time."

"Did you feel pain?"

"No, oh no, I was out my physical body, but still connected to it. I was very close by watching all that was going on but I think the most interesting thing that there were people on the scene within minutes, but I think it was the ones that were instantly there that are most interesting to people because they are the ones that disappeared from the scene. I understand them to have been the people responsible for our passing. Particularly two gentlemen, who were equally desperately not administering first aid but as it were searching through, sort of, how do I say…"

"Belongings?"

"Like a body search, looking for, well, I suppose evidence of some description they were after physical, or the removal of anything sort of, incriminating, that is when they removed Dodi's ring, because I, I was, although my physical body was unconscious of course the spiritual one is very much awake. Being in close proximity you can sense all that. It's very odd because immediately as you leave the body you are very aware of the physical condition, but the longer you erm, and I don't mean the body, I mean the physical plane of existence. You are very aware of the physical plane of existence but as you stay there a little bit longer it does all sort of start to fade away. It is really because your body naturally elevates to the spirit world or a lot of people will call it the etheric plane where most people, as far as I know, most people on their passing, go to in the first instance, almost like one of those clearing houses."

"Like a hospital?"

"Not necessarily, it depends again on the person's circumstances of their passing. Mine was a little bit different because I was aware very much because I could see what had happened in the crash, and therefore was very, very aware of the crash and the circumstances and could see that there was no way our physical bodies would be able to sustain the spirit afterwards.

"When I, as it were, became aware of the Spirit world I didn't travel down a white tunnel of light. It is as if the one scene faded away from view, and another came into view. I was met by, well there were several people came to meet me."

"Who was the first person that you saw?"

"Oddly enough there was a lady who was dressed as a nurse but it was a very old fashioned nurses uniform that she was wearing, so that sort of took me a bit by surprise. She was immediately on the scene from the Spirit world, and she said to me 'you don't need to hang around here dear'. Which I thought was rather quaint being called 'dear', having been called your Royal Highness and Princess Diana, for someone to address me as 'dear' was quite nice really."

"Kind of normal?"

"Yes! To be just spoken to as if you are just another person, it was actually quite nice. Anyway this lovely nurse led me away and I was offered the opportunity to rest in the Spirit hospital. Of course in reality I didn't need to, but you just do as you're told don't you?"

"Do you?"

"Well, someone says well you have had a nasty accident my dear, come with me and we'll just make you rest for a little while.

So I was taken into this hospital area, of course it didn't really occur to me that my body, as far as I was concerned my physical body, but it was my spirit body, was perfectly all right, but I was extremely tired. I was later given a bed to lie down on, and went off to sleep. Later on, I do not know how long, but I don't think it was very long, I woke and there were people whose faces I recognised but I couldn't quite place them, because I thought, 'but that's, that's my grandmother, and yet she's dead, what is she doing here? It was very odd, it was odd, and then this wonderful nurse was still nearby. I didn't talk to my grandmother, because I thought I was going mad. I said to the nurse I think I must have had a knock on the head. She laughed and said, 'Why do you say that dear?' I said Well I'm sure I can see my grandmother sitting over there. The nurse laughed again and she said 'but dear that is your grandmother', but I said 'she's dead' and the nurse just looked me and smiled and she said, 'my dear do you not realise what has happened to you?' and I said, well I know I was in a crash and I could see everything very clearly, but what has happened? She said 'Well you've passed on yourself!'

"Wow, and you didn't realise that at the time Diana?"

"Well on one level, I suppose you do, because when I think of it now the awareness of being out of my body and seeing my body in the car was one thing, but not to associate it with well that the body and I were in some way connected. It was a really odd thing, it was as if that was somebody else but of course it was the physical part."

"Is it a frightening experience or is it a very peaceful experience?"

"Well of course the accident itself appears to be quite traumatic, but it really was quite instantaneous, in the way that both of us were out of our bodies, so in terms of physical pain there really wasn't that. So you would have to say in the most strange way it was actually quite calm, it's almost as if when the impact took place, there is this great peace that descends."

"I think that will be of great comfort to people reading this, not just from the point of when you passed but for themselves and their own losses."

"There's a sense of at first maybe you're aware because as my physical body was still conscious there were sounds that I could hear, but could not respond to that were obviously of the earth condition. At the same time I am able to see, with what I understand to have been my spirit body, watching all that was taking place. It was just a most odd, but very interesting as I look at it now, I see how interesting it all is. It's so sad that so many people do not understand that they are not just one, but two of you, there is your spirit that animates the physical body, and though they are joined together they are… you know it is quite such a strange concept for a lot of people to understand. The way I am given to understand it is as they say you are spirit in a body."

"That's right, and you're just using it, for what you need to use it for."

"It's a very interesting thing for people to know and understand, and I hope it will be of some comfort to others who have lost people in road incidents."

"Or even in shocking situations, like murder."

"I think it is important for people to understand that er, I cannot say that nobody feels any pain, that would be wrong. What I can say, the pain that people may experience is a very brief, very fleeting, brief thing, because it relates to the physical body and not the spirit. Therefore no matter how macabre or hideous the results of an incident may appear the reality is that very little pain is actually experienced by the victim."

"What about the cancer sufferers? You worked with lots of people who were very ill. How does that work if you have cancer, how does that work when you pass?

"I am just asking <Diana spoke to other spirit workers>, because I have been to visit a few people here."

" That you knew?"

" Oh yes, some of those lovely people I met who later passed on, and I've made it part of my wish to make contact with them and see how they are doing. You know I have spoken to different people and asked them their experiences because I think it's interesting to understand how it works for different people and in different circumstances. But actually there is a great similarity, at the moment when the spirit is ready to leave the physical body, there is often very much a sense of complete and utter peace. I think this is often reflected in the physical body because people often say, I went to see so and so in the chapel of rest and they had this peaceful look on their face.

"As the spirit withdraws there is no need for the body to endure pain and suffering any more and therefore it is in reality at peace, and I think that's very much reflected on the faces of those who have passed when they are seen in a chapel of rest.

"They often look quite different from the person who was maybe struggling to breathe because the person had lung cancer or whatever, the appearance is often much more peaceful, and I think in some ways that's quite a helpful thing because then people realise that the suffering is now over. Even if they do not recognise the reality of the spirit living after death, if they go and see the physical body and the peaceful look, then that can bring a lot of comfort to people. I am not advocating everyone rushes to their local chapel of rest, but if that is the way that it will bring them comfort then I think it can be of use. What else can I tell you?"

"I think it's very interesting what you say about the moment that you passed and what you experienced, can I backtrack a little bit about that moment and ask you if you know who those people were, not in the sense of their organisation, but who they actually were, in the sense of their name?"

"Oh the individuals you mean? When you think of what happens at the time of such an incident, your instant concern is whether you are going to recover or find out what your situation is, and you don't necessarily dwell too much at the time on those things, but they were very clearly to me at the time these two gentlemen. One was constantly calling the other one Phil, but I'm not sure whether that was his name or it was just the name they used between the two of them, but it was Phil this and Phil that. What can I give you in terms of evidence?"

"I suppose what it is Diana is from the point of view of the layman, the reader, including John and I is to give as much evidence as possible."

"One of them I know, is connected to MI6, although I do not believe that his superiors know of his involvement, because he is clearly a member of this other organisation but he equally, you could almost call him a double agent, but he's supposedly working for the British causes and equally runs on the second agenda of how it stands now of Queen and country, I am led to understand that the name 'Phil' is just a code name. One that he is commonly called, it is like his operative name that is used."

"Well, that's very interesting," I replied. "They are interesting people that don't give much away about themselves and kind of lead double lives even though they are quite honest."

"I think there are things going on in MI6 and other secret organisations, that even those that are in charge would be quite shocked to understand what is going on. The amount of infiltration and double infiltration is really quite staggering, and although they will protest when the contents of this is produced, you wait and see, they will find several moles within, and these need to be sorted out because it is not, clearly in the interests of Queen and country for these people to be doing the sort of things they are, and they desperately need to be sorted out."

"Diana, do you know, it's changing the subject a little bit, do you know where Osama Bin Laden would have gone, do you know if he has been executed?"

"I don't know, I am sorry I don't know, who is this man?" replied Diana

"He is the leader of a terrorist group called Al Queda, you know all the troubles in the Middle East?"

"Oh, I see, I will try and find out, let me see <*Again a consultation with other spirit workers*>"

"I wonder how he would learn from that."

"I am just asking some of the other people here, and they tell me he is actually still alive, at this moment in time, what is it December 2006? He is still alive, but he is very much like a rat caught in a trap at the moment."

"So are they going to execute him or not?"

"It is very difficult, you cannot always predict what exactly is going to happen, the simple reason is that what you see in terms of looking forward here are possibilities, so there is a possibility very much that he will be caught and brought to justice and face some sort of, I am going to say kangaroo court, because that's exactly what it would be. Equally it's very possible that someone who's a little bit trigger happy shall we say will say he tried to escape and kill him, so there are a couple of options that are possible at the moment."

"I think he would do well to stay on the earth plane to learn and understand about what suffering he has brought to people," I stated.

"I have had to very quickly ask whilst you are talking and asking these questions, because I don't really have any knowledge of this person. I am led to believe that he is a very unsavoury character, and like all unsavoury characters he will have to pay a price at some point. It is so sad to see how the earth plane reacts in ways of violence to deal with those they consider to be criminal and what they do in reality is thrust them out of the physical body, and unfortunately those ones that are of that ilk are very attached to the earth plane usually and tend to just hang around and they can of course influence others of like mind. Instead of actually getting rid of a problem you can actually have caused another one, because they could then motivate someone else to even far worse things than they were capable of on the earth plane. Ridding the earth plane of someone in that way is not always the best way. Far better, as you would say, to keep them on the earth plane and bring them to some understanding of the immensity of their crimes that so upset the world. Surely it must be more of a punishment to keep them in a regimented way of life, rather than set them free by releasing them from their body, how ridiculous it is to kill!"

"I work with children and families, and always when you get a murderer that's really angry and aggressive, and you look at their childhood and you look at where they have come from you can really piece it together and find answers. I think that's more helpful, you know?"

"You know the trouble is, Diana said, it all boils down to money, it's far cheaper to put a rope around someone's neck or a bullet in their chest, than to keep them accommodated and alive for 30 years. Not that they should ever be released, I don't believe that that would serve any useful purpose.

"What they also do by killing these people, and it is just killing, they may try and quantify it by saying it's justified, because the powers in control that have arranged it, but it is still murder, it is still killing, it makes the governments or the powers concerned no better than the killers themselves."

"Precisely! But not everyone holds that view," I replied.

"What would be far better is to have that person kept on the earth plane for them to even make in some small way because they can never return for some of the things they do, not in this existence, but it would help, if they could be shown some of the things they have done and also to prepare them for life in the Spirit world where they will at some point will have to deal with, and face the consequences of their actions you know. I must very, very quickly; I really would like to speak a little bit on landmines. Obviously there is very little that I can do from the Spirit world, where I live now to campaign and get others involved, but it is so important, you know so many children are still being maimed by these awful devices, and they really shouldn't be used in warfare they are just brutal killing machines, that have no discernment against who is an enemy and who is an innocent, they just kill indiscriminately and it really should be brought to the world's attention, and I call upon the people of not just England, but of the world, to demand that these awful devices be stopped being produced and being used in warfare. That is all I wanted to say, but I feel so passionately even now, and we have places here where we deal with people who have suffered the traumas of the devastation to the physical of these things, but they also have a psychological impact as well, so not only when they come to Spirit, of course their body, as far as the spirit is concerned is full again, but psychologically the damage can last beyond the grave, and these people still have to be helped. The same thing applies to those who have committed these sorts of offences we were just talking about. If they were like, as you say, a homicidal maniac, what do people think happens to them just because they are released out of their body that they suddenly become angelic? Of course they don't!

They survive death the same as everybody else, but they still hold onto those homicidal tendencies they had and what have you done? You've just set a Spirit loose so it can attach itself, or get close to someone else and cause more problems."

Once again the time came for us to part ways; there was much more I wanted to ask Diana, but I would have to wait for another occasion for us to speak some more, as always I could hardly wait. It wasn't to be a long wait; the following day offered an opportunity for me to talk further to Diana.

8 DIANA'S RECOVERY

"I did tell you about my initial adventure as I came to the Spirit world and how I was met, and several people who'd passed over before me were there to greet me in the hospital environment. So it will be best if I continue from that point of the story is that okay?"

"Yes, that will be fine."

"I was not in the hospital very long, really you'd be amazed how quickly one can move on from such a location. The idea of physical injury is a strange one to us in the spirit because you cannot hurt the spiritual body as you can the physical one. Therefore the time for recuperation is much less than it would be on the physical plane, it's a completely different thing. So within a very short space of time, I would say, well, within a matter of hours really, once I understood that I was fit and well, you see I did have an advantage of course because I had knowledge of the spiritual nature of the human soul, which is well known about of course. So it was easier to explain to me than it is to others, some people don't even need to go at all to a hospital of any description in the Spirit world because their knowledge is such that it is totally irrelevant. Others need a longer period of recuperation and coming to terms with their condition. It does vary from person to person, they don't all end up in a hospital, they don't all find themselves in that location when they pass, but that was my story, that was my story. So, well I was obviously as such fit and well to leave the hospital and be led to my new environment, and it was lovely. It would be very difficult for people to understand the difference, but my life was such that people would worship me and chase me for photographs. One got used to it, but it could be very irritating. To be in this new dimension, where I am just accepted as being just the same as everyone else, with no greater or lesser importance, but allowed to be free, something I had not experienced for many, many years. Funny, isn't it strange, that we should really share a background you and I where we both were in a caring profession of looking after children, and this is wonderful that I can speak to someone who is not only sensitive but has an understanding of that type of work. Of course we digress from what we were talking about. So I was taken from the hospital and at first I went to live with my grandmother and we shared a very simple home, not like the grandeur that I was used to on the earth plane. It was a very comfortable very practical location, very peaceful with beautiful gardens, wonderful floral decorations in the garden, beautiful flowers I cannot begin to describe, even the grass was as green as green could be, even to actually describe it is very difficult, because there isn't sort of the moisture and the mud you would connect with grass on the earth plane, it is of a much springier feel to it I guess also because the body is so much lighter, you literally feel as if you can glide across it and not quite make contact, and it's very peaceful and very relaxed. So I spent a little time, I suppose you could call it further recuperation, but I think now of it as a period of adjustment where I was allowed to just find my own way and just to 'be' which is something I had not been allowed to do for a long, long time.

"So that was wonderful but then of course having been so involved in supporting charitable work, and it really was and became a passion for me on earth, to work for charities and promote the issues that really should be important rather than which country are we going to bomb next, it should be which person are we going to help next."

"Do you have association with NCH, National Children's Home/Charity? That's who I work for."

"It is another wonderful charity and I was a supporter of many, many charities. Unfortunately I could not always be a supporter of every one that asked me, and that was always a concern for me because they all are in need of desperate help and support, but there is only so much that one can do. It wasn't possible to attend every charitable function you were asked to do."

"I wonder if when the book comes out that it may be of help to them?"

"Well, I would like to think it might, but I think if it helps any charity if just the words, or the idea that Diana is still supporting charities from the Spirit side of life, I hope it is of use to all charities, especially my real love is for children, and I would love to see all those charitable organisations working for the best interests of children getting all the support they possibly can. So I do share that passion for those. Obviously as I said before about my passion for the removal of items such as landmines and all sorts of horrible booby trap bombs, but all those things need to be highlighted and be taken seriously by the politicians ruling the countries, and if one of them was brave enough to stand up and say we will not use these as weapons, then maybe the rest would follow, and once and for all we would remove these horrible things."

Diana continued with her story by saying, "So I spent a little time with my grandmother, and then I decided it would be nice for me to just have my own little place not a very big house at all, but it is a house, and I have my own gardens filled with beautiful flowers, and for a little while I was quite happy with that. You know I felt I really needed a break from all this sort of constant movement and getting involved in things. It was for a very short time then I started to be visited by different people in the Spirit world some that you would know of."

" For example?"

"Oh some you have spoken to, Winston Churchill for one. Can you imagine that, I mean I know people would think of me as someone quite famous, but to open your door one day and find Winston Churchill standing there is really rather strange. But he needed to meet me because he wanted to explain what had happened and felt quite strongly that these people need to be brought to account. So he sort of sat with me and we had some very long discussions, about what I remembered, about what he had been able to discover himself and he introduced several others that have been involved in talking, you know we spoke, well not I, but others of our group that have come together and spoken to you about Dodi and I meeting again which we did, and continue to do so, although we are not together as such here in the spirit world."

"Why is that Diana, why when you had such a love and adoration for each other why are you not together now?"

"We come together when the wish and desire is to do so, we each get on with our own particular life but that is no different from the earth plane, there were times when we could not be together through engagements or whatever, and Dodi is himself very busy in the Spirit world, and he has become more passionate about things he realises are wrong on the earth plane, so he is very involved in trying to help people reach some sort of understanding and work in that way. I equally do my part and I talk to people here in the Spirit world about the difficulties groups and organisations on the earth plane have with them in terms of raising funds or having the right people to work within them even. Some people are very spiritually motivated with the best of intentions and then you only have to have one who comes along to really feather their own nest, it can really disrupt a charity and cause it such terrible problems. So there are some here that are involved in trying to help keep these organisations on an even keel, and doing the work that they have set out to do. I am very involved now in not only still trying to do what I can to help and encourage and influence the thinking of some of the charities that I had been involved with but equally to influence, you know, politicians. You know when I was on the earth plane you couldn't really speak to a politician in case you were accused of allegiance to one party or another. But I think really party politics is largely irrelevant in the spirit world."

"I think it's quite relevant here!"

"What happens from our aspect is what is the best for the people? Therefore we will try and influence whoever who is going to make it best for the people. So it is quite different from the earthly systems.

"It feels here that it's very much about control obviously, and about the power and control of trying to manipulate people. Equally I feel that religion, and I am probably going to get shot down about this, but I feel that religion is the same, control and power you know?

"I have to giggle and smile to myself a little because well, they could try and shoot me down, but you know as I am already over here it is a bit difficult for them. I would agree with you, there is too much power, and abuse of power that connects between the church and politics in general. It really should be broken apart; it's very interesting that you mention the orthodox churches, because they have played a certain role in the incident relating to Dodi and myself. You see there are a lot of people in the religious arena, some of who would be absolutely horrified to know what is done in their name, but others who believe they are acting in God's name.
"Because you know you've only got to be led to believe that God has instructed that you do this or that, and that therefore no matter how horrendous the act is, they will act it out, and this was part and parcel of our removal shall I say. There was great religious input being placed in certain quarters."

"In what sense Diana?"

"In the sense that there were those that believed I would be a very serious threat to the monarchy, and more importantly, a serious threat should I carry a child from a second marriage. How ridiculous was that as an idea!!"

"But also the fact that you were considering marrying a Muslim, you know that's it isn't it?"

"Of course, that must be the ultimate insult, so there was a vested interest from the religious point of view, to see us removed out of the picture. As you say you may well be shot down, or attempted to be shot down, but the reality is that there was influence and remains influence within the orthodox churches, not just the Church of England and the Catholic Church. Particularly those two I would say, their influence is very strong within the various denominations, and the lobbying that takes place quite frankly is quite inappropriate sometimes."

"Diana, I meet lots of people and they're very much focussed around fear with religion. You can't do this, you shouldn't do this, and if you do this you're going to hell, if you do this there is not going to be a place for you, and I think it's a real shame that people live their life like that, living under that cloak of fear. To me God or whatever is to be welcomed into your life rather than to be afraid of."

"You have a very good understanding of things, but there are many people who do not, and therein lies the problem, because what you know to be the truth, and what I understood to be the truth is far removed from the vast majority of people in the United Kingdom, and they are very much ruled through fear, as you say if you do not do this you will go to hell, but if you give half your money to the church you will go to heaven. You and I know that that's a ridiculous concept, you know as Jesus said, 'it is easier for a camel to pass through the eye of a needle than for a rich man to enter the kingdom of heaven'. The same applies to those of the church, the financial and political power that they hold here will not entitle any churchman to pass to the kingdom of heaven, just because they swore some man made oath to God, it really doesn't add up at all."

"When we look at the teenagers that we have today and the violence and the fear and anger that is happening in society with teenagers. When I look at them I just see the fear in their eyes, I don't necessarily see someone who is an aggressor I see somebody who is very, very afraid, and I think society has developed that, through the fear of what's going to happen in life you know?"

"I think there are a couple of things here. One is the fear-based aspects of religion, which is causing great problems, but then there is also this rather ridiculous, I hate to say the words nanny state, this ridiculous nanny state where you know, you mustn't do this to a child because it is an infringement of this right or that right, and sometimes children really do need to be directed. I do not mean through violence or aggression, that is not the way, but through guidance. But to just allow a child to run riot because it might breach their rights in some way is ridiculous isn't it?"

"I think if we can start young, if we can start thinking about setting boundaries and understanding about how safe and secure children can feel if they have got those boundaries, they just feel completely omnipotent and completely insecure if they have no boundaries, and then you find you have a child that is just crazy, and won't do anything you ask them, because you don't mean what you say, and they know you don't mean what you say."

"Then you have an uncontrollable situation. This is what I am about, is that there needs to be a change in the way these things are approached, there is too much concern about law, and not enough about the social practicalities and guidance that these children desperately want."

"And Diana, the emotional containing of what they are feeling. We look at setting rules for children, but it's not about that. It's about giving them a sense that you understand them and when they are upset, or angry or frustrated and then from that, helping them to understand why you set the boundaries, you know?"

"Exactly, exactly."

"Because if we don't look at emotions and help them with that, how can we help them with anything else?"

"It will be interesting to see what people think of these words won't it? Maybe somebody somewhere will say, well that makes sense, I think we should look at this in a different way, we should turn away from this idea of let's legislate about this, that and another, but look at it in what is really the best possible way for us to move forward to provide a safe society for our children."

"So the people feel safe within it (society)."

"People feel safe, for the children to develop properly. These are going to be your custodians when you are older. If you have not set the boundaries, and they are uncontrollable now, goodness knows what they are going to do to you when you are older!"

"Well Diana, what about the fact that the children we've got now are going to be parents? That's a scary thought when I think of some of the children I am working with right now."

"It is a real issue that needs to be addressed very, very urgently, otherwise there will be many more problems for er particularly the UK, but you see unfortunately a lot of the other countries in the world look towards the UK as we are considered a leader in the so called civilised world. If our example is to say, well yes you can have uncontrollable children running riot, what are we doing for the rest of the planet?"

"What model are we giving?"

"Worse still, as I say if these children, which they will, become leaders of the world one day. What is to stop them waging war and continuing the violence and vicious cycles that we have currently in place? So I think there is very much to consider. Anyway I must wrap things up a little bit, and bring it back, really that it was what I have been doing here in what you call the spirit world. I have spent a little time getting adjusted to my circumstances, and now I am back campaigning as it were, but in a far more quiet way, that a lot of people will never know about, but I try and use my influence in every way I can, so that the best that can be achieved for the people, the users and end users of the charities will receive the best possible of what that charity can do, and I hope others will take up the reigns and carry on that work. Others of note I hope will actually allow their names even just their names, to be put to a charity, it is just that simple act that can really help a charity move itself forward. Which is why I did try and work or offer my name to charities as I said I couldn't always attend every event or in some cases I couldn't attend any events. But it was enough for them to know that I was there and would support if I could. Well that is my life to date, but now I feel it very necessary, as I have spoken with Dodi and Winston and others, that this story comes out of what happened, and to give the people an idea of what is going on beneath the façade of civilised government, and the very real efforts of those in government who are trying to do the right thing, and I don't necessarily mean any particular party when I say this, but those who are representative of the public, they need to also be aware that there are groups undermining their very efforts, and I think that's a very important message as well."

Diana told me she needed to withdraw, and we said our farewells, but our session was not over, Jimmy Jones had come to join us once again. I greeted Jimmy with the words:

"It's nice to speak to you again."

"It's very interesting, what you have been talking about. I think it will give a lot of people a lot of things to think about."

"I think it's lovely that Diana and I share the same passion, and we have the same background of working with children."

"It makes it easier for us in Spirit when we try and talk to people, if we have some sort of connection. It doesn't have to be a love connection, which I think a lot of people think it has to be. If you share the same thoughts and ideals that is just as strong a connection as any love connection, and if you start to become friends as a result of it, it's lovely!"

"So how are you doing?"

"I'm fine, I'm fine, I'm doing alright."

"We're going to be partying tonight, New Years Eve."

"Yes, I reckon you'll have a good laugh, and good on you, because you both deserve a little break. You know I think we ought to sort of leave things there for now. If that's alright with you?"

"Well I'd like to talk to you more but…"

"I'd love to talk, I love to talk, after all I volunteered for this job as well."

"Jimmy can I just ask you a question?"

"Yes."

"Yesterday I asked about Osama Bin Laden, have you heard of him?"

"Well I have now! Because I was present when he was being talked about."

"I didn't mean to say him, I meant to say Saddam Hussein."

"That's fine, that's fine. But actually you needed to talk about him that was our influence if you like. So we were a bit naughty but…"

"We saw the newspapers today, and Saddam Hussein has been killed now, is he up there? With you?"

"Blimey, he's not with me, that's for sure! From what I gather, he's not a nice sort of bloke at all. He will have gravitated to the part of the Spirit world that he has created for himself. It isn't, from what I understand, a very nice place. It's a very dark sad place, but it's not like, you get preached a hell of fire and brimstone, it's not that sort, it's a hell of their own creation, it can be a very dreary dull place. Because of how far he has retreated he will be like many others of that sort of mind set, where he'll almost be in a place of isolation, but at some point, he will get opportunities to step out and move forward. I know that is difficult for some people to understand."

"I really hope that happens!"

"I think it's also important that people understand that no matter how bad someone is, or considered to be, they always, in the afterlife have an opportunity to move forward. There is always for everybody, no matter what you think you've done that's so bad, an opportunity for you to move forward. But you do have to make amends for all the acts."

"All of them?"

" Everything, there is no escape, you don't get sort of let off."

"Is it also for your thoughts as well Jimmy? Because what I understand is that every thought is noted within you? Does that make sense?"

"Well, yeah, because every thought is energy in action, but the trouble with a lot of thoughts is that they don't always do what you think they would do. If you have a negative thought about someone, it doesn't necessarily hurt them. What often happens is that it bounces back to you. Instead of the person getting what you are wishing for them, it comes to you instead. The best way to attack, if you like, someone who has hurt you, is to surround them with love."

"Absolutely, that's the hardest thing to do sometimes here on the earth plane."

"Of course it is, you think how I felt, there was that bloke that gunned me down, instantly my reaction was you know, I want to get him somehow. I knew quickly that that wasn't the best thing to do, but it was my instant reaction, but he was just doing his job, just as I was. In truth, and we've met since, at the time you want to get him, you want revenge. But revenge doesn't solve anything, what you need to do is understand why, and take the lesson away with you, so you can move forward."

"Wise words!"

"Maybe, maybe, but I really do have to go now I am afraid, talk to you next year they say!"

"Next year is tomorrow!"

"Well that ain't far away then is it? We'll talk to you next year, well you know people say, are they aware of time in the Spirit world? We don't have time like you know it, because of our connection with you, and what's going on here we're very aware of your time scale at the moment, so we are very aware of that."

"Bless you."

"Bless you as well," Jimmy said and then he departed, presumably back to his home in the Spirit realms.

9 NEW YEAR, NEW CONVERSATION

A few days later on the 2nd of January 2007, we once again sat so that Spirit could continue with their story. John was becoming reluctant to sit, but with a bit of persuasion he once again allowed himself to be used by Spirit, and our conversation started firstly with Chin Lee, and is written here to give the reader an understanding of what takes place on occasion with an entranced medium.

" Good evening!" I said, greeting Chin Lee.

"Good evening to you child, it is good to be with you again. I know the instrument <Chin Lee's description of John> is very reluctant to work sometimes and needs, how you say, a good kick up the behind!"

"Well you could say push. I encourage him though."

"Yes, we get there in the end. Well I have just very quickly stepped in just to say 'Hello' and check that things are settled with the instrument. I am going to hand over to young Jimmy, and I will let him conduct the rest of the conversations this evening. If time allows and the instrument does not fight too much I may come back and talk. We'll see what happens okay? Well have a very good evening child, I am sure you will have a lot of questions to ask."

"I don't have any at the moment, but I am sure as soon as Jimmy talks to me I will."

"Well you understand as well that we in the Spirit world wish for certain information to come out, and that is why you will also find that you are fed sometimes, questions or ideas of what to ask, but do not worry, it's so that we can assist in bringing out the information that we think is necessary for people to hear. Okay, well as I say, have a very good evening child, I will leave you with the very cheeky Jimmy."

Chin Lee stepped back and once again we were joined by Jimmy Jones.

"Hi there Jimmy!"

"Oh, Hello, it's been interesting eh, all those people you've been talking to?"

"Yes, very interesting, we're very excited."

"It's an interesting story, that's for sure. We've got much more to put down haven't we?"

"Yes, and we've got little time to do it, so I keep encouraging John to try and sit down."

"Well, where was we? I forgot where we was!"

"You popped in for a little while after Diana. You just popped in and you said you wanted to come back. We were talking about lots of things really, we were talking about Osama Bin Laden, and that situation."

"Yeah, interesting ain't it, when people you consider, or are labelled 'evil' people, it's very interesting to understand that as you say, something similar happens to them as happens to everyone else. If they are truly, I don't want to say the word 'evil' cos it's not correct, but if their thinking is such that they do create the conditions where they will live in the Spirit world, and they can't escape it! Whereas you can escape the justice of your world, you can't ever escape the justice of ours. So there is always that payback."

"Is that you as a soul, and I don't mean you personally, but when you pass over, my understanding is that you judge yourself?"

"Well you do in a way, that's right, you're helped, but it's not like you're forced to do it. But it's something you are definitely encouraged, and all of us at some point go through that review. What you do, you have access to the records, they call them the Akashic records, and the Akashic records in plain language is a record of everything that has ever happened. You can see your whole life played back in detail. You make the judgement. Others may help you to look at certain aspects and say 'do you think you really did the best you could there' or equally 'don't you think you're being a bit hard on yourself there'. You are your worst judge you know. Judging yourself is the hardest thing you know, because we all tend to judge ourselves far more critically than others would. Anyway I suppose we ought to talk about the story, we do go off on a tangent don't we, and much as I love talking about all that. So we'd brought Diana to you, and she filled you in a bit of detail about the incident from her perspective, her life going forward after that. That was very interesting as well, lovely for even some of us to hear you know? Well mine was slightly different, when I passed over to Spirit, when I was shot down, I was met by a sergeant major, and it was just really weird, cos I remember sort of being hit, and you don't really realise you do cos it's so quick. I was just lying on the battlefield amongst all this smoke of the battle, but the weird thing was that the battle sounded like it was far away. Then I noticed several other soldiers starting to stand up, you know, amongst the smoke, all looking like me, pretty bewildered, wondering what had happened, what happened to the battle, and then this sergeant major comes along and says' 'right lads, follow me.' So you do as you're told when you are in the army, so we just followed him. We were taken to some barracks and our names were checked off on a list just like you were expected in the army. Then we were given opportunities just to get used to the environment, and gradually, one by one we were told what had happened. You realised then that you had passed on."

"I suppose from your point of view, being in the army that would have been the best way, because you would have taken more notice of that, instead of an angel appearing saying 'come with me'."

"Blimey, think we'd have all run away if we'd seen an angel! This way it was something we were familiar with, and it just seems natural. Well, it is all natural, that's the thing, it is all natural. So you find the environment that you first go into, is something that you would feel comfortable in.

"If you worked on the buses, you might find that there is a bus that you can get on. So if you felt comfortable about it you'd get on it and then you would find someone would help you from there. It depends on your own circumstances, and the way you think. All those different ways in which you could pass are looked after."

"So it would be relative to the experience you'd had on the earth plane?"

"Yes, people are helped."

"There are a lot of thoughts people have about what actually happens Jimmy, so I think that should be a great comfort to many people."

"Do you know what? What makes us laugh is the idea people have of if you've been good you're going to go to heaven, and play a harp, and equally ridiculous is the idea of a place of fiery brimstone. You have to understand it's all about fear and control.

Part of our job here, apart from telling an interesting story that people will want to hear about, is to give them that understanding of what will happen to them when they pass over. So we can start to remove some of the fear, and when you can start to do that then people can start to understand that passing on is just a continuation. It will hopefully get them to start thinking about what they are actually doing where you live. About how they can work and behave differently, and create a better place to live in."

"Gosh! I do hope that starts to happen Jimmy."

"I think you'll see that this work we are doing will have quite an impact, as I've said we've been working on this for quite sometime. We're just getting this to a stage where it can all be written down and published."

Jimmy then brought us back to the main story of our book, and began to introduce a new visitor to us. By saying the following:
"This is quite a strange character really, cos you might think, hang on a minute where does this one come from?"

"See if you can send the thoughts to me, and I'll see…"

"No, I don't want you to guess, I'll tell you who he is. He was considered very much a leader amongst his people in fact he did run his country more or less for a while, and was very important in gaining independence for India. His name, you know him as Ghandi, and he's waiting to talk. So let me leave you with Ghandi, and I am sure you will have a very interesting conversation, cos he won't speak how you think he would. Do you have any idea of him?"

"No I don't have any conception or thought about him."

"A lot of people have preconceptions about how someone will speak, coming from this place or that place, but he's different, he's different, but you'll have a very interesting conversation, so I'll leave you with him but I won't be back today, but I'm just gonna let Ghandi have a word or two and then we'll see what happens after that eh? I'll come back and talk another time. Well you have a nice chat anyway."

10 GHANDI & VLADIMIR

After Jimmy's introduction I waited in anticipation, soon I was joined by Ghandi speaking through John.

"You must bear with me, it is er, I am just trying to adjust to this, it is very um, what word do I use? It is as if you are talking through a very thick piece of cloth or something."

"Can you hear me okay?"

"I can hear you, but I am not able to see anything at the moment. Did you know that I was educated in England?"

"No I didn't."

"It is why I have this…"

"Beautiful accent!"

"Yes, I was able to communicate on many levels, but obviously being able to speak English was of great benefit because I could talk and argue the cause of what I felt was right for my country of India, much better than some of my fellows who had not had the opportunity to gain the knowledge and fluency of the English language. So I wonder where I can add into this story, because you would understand that where I was located was a far cry away from the incident of Diana and Dodi, which obviously is of great interest to the British population."

Ghandi paused briefly and continued, "You will find records relating to an attempt on my life before I passed away in more reasonable circumstances. But there was an attempt on my life by the same group of individuals."

<It should be noted here that Mahatma Ghandi was assassinated by being shot at point blank range on 30th January 1948. His words 'reasonable circumstances' seem ironic to say the least, yet compared to other attempts on his life it could be argued that being shot was a more reasonable way to die than any other.>

"And this is documented Ghandi?"

"Yes, all this is documented. Luckily of course they failed, and it was very much attempted to be covered up as being by some extremist group. Of course that really wasn't the reality. It was these individuals supposedly fighting for King and country."

Our communication paused at this point and I waited to see if Ghandi would talk again. A few minutes later he recommenced our interview.

"The aborted plan took place in Delhi, and I was supposed to be killed by a bomb planted on the side of the road. But it failed to go off at the exact moment it should have done."

"Did it kill other people?"

"There were other people injured and I believe there was a fatality there but it was none of my particular entourage. It was a poor innocent bystander, but of course it was documented at the time, but carefully brushed away as the work of an extremist organisation, but in effect I suppose you could say it was this sort of paramilitary group who thought I was a threat to the British Empire, and should be 'taken out' accordingly. Thankfully they failed, and India was granted its independence, and after it was granted independence there was no real need to pursue that course of action to remove me from the picture. It's just another piece in the jigsaw puzzle of what has been happening over the years. I must point out that is not the same individuals, but the same organisation that has continued over the years. When you think of the amount of your earth time that has gone by, it would not be possible for the same individuals. But this is an organisation that has carefully recruited personnel and as others have reached a time when they felt, shall we say, it right to retire, others have picked up the mantle and gone forward with it."

"So it's constantly being renewed in a sense?"

"Constantly being revised, constantly being recruited, constantly fighting for information, much of which is confidential of course, but some of these people are involved with secret intelligence services in your country. I think the message is even wider than this, and that is that many countries in the world have very similar things going on. Where there are people willing to undermine the democratically persons and will even take to the extremes of taking out those that they think are deemed a threat, whoever that may be, it is obviously a cause for concern, but by highlighting the issue it does give those who are democratically elected the opportunity to wheedle these undesirables out, and let the full force of democracy really have its sway. Those people are elected, whether you like them or not, to represent the people and they should be allowed to do that and not be undermined in any way shape or form."

"What year was the attempt made on your life?"

"Nineteen fifty nine, no, erm I can't remember, I'm not sure if it was the late 1950s." <*again just a reminder Ghandi was assassinated in January 1948, so this statement is of great interest and concern*>

Ghandi continued, "I get a little bit confused. There was another attempt on my life but not by this group, that was by gunshot, but that was later."

"In the late 1950s?" I asked not knowing myself at this point when Ghandi had passed.

"It was earlier than that, I can't quite remember."

"So in what year did you actually pass?" I persisted.

My question was met with silence, and it was some time before I got a further response.

"The early 1960s, I never was any good with dates."

"How did you pass?"

" I passed with cancer."

"In what organ?"

"In the liver. Then it spread and there was nothing anyone could have done. It seems rather funny that there were those attempts to take my life, and cancer succeeds where they failed." <*Again historically, Ghandi did not, according to our research have cancer, and died as a result of an assassination attempt on 30th January 1948, clearly we were either now talking to someone else, or if this was truly Ghandi, something was very much awry.* >

Our communicator continued, "My part in this is really rather small. My interest is in letting people know that these people not only operate not just in their localised countries, but if you consider my existence and my work in India, and where these people were operating then, the fact that they could operate quite freely, even in the more recent years in France, really without impedement I think is of interest to a lot of people, and the fact that this group is in existence even today.

"It is time for all those who are engaged in such activities to be exposed. Not just the British public, but the world population need to know that they can trust that those who are ruling the country, really are running the country, and those that seek to undermine the democratic processes, should be treated as the criminals and terrorists that they actually are.

"Well I don't think I have anything further to add for now. I don't know if there will be any need for me to come back. Of course feel free, I would like to be of help if I can. Really my little piece was to make people aware of how widespread really such activity takes place. You know I was renowned for being a man of peace. That is also part of my driving force now, is to bring true peace to the people, and there is still so much going on, even in my country, let alone yours or others. If we can all unite in some way then we can start to bring changes about so that people can live without fear of reprisal. It is absolutely ridiculous, the types of activity that goes on."

"What's your view on Saddam Hussein, and what's just happened recently with Saddam Hussein?"

My question was met with silence. Clearly our communicator seemed to be checking with others in the Spirit realms before returning to speak.

"I was just asking here who this gentleman was."

"Not really a gentleman."

"It's just a term of phrase, I don't like putting labels, negative labels to people, as there are equal amounts in us that are able to be the good, positive person, and the aspects that can make us act in ways that others would consider to be evil.

"So I try not to label as being bad or good. I do not have any real knowledge of this gentleman, which may sound strange to a lot of people because I understand he is of quite relevance in today's news, and in what has been going on just recently. You have to understand that in our world that people of that type are not really topic of great news or conversation. We are far more interested in those who have been hurt by such actions. Those that perpetrate them, have to face up to that at some point, and often they are not willing to be helped when they first arrive here. So our main focus will be on individuals who you may never hear of, or know of, but how they are helped to adapt to what has happened and to their new surroundings.

"I am really sorry but I really do have to step back, as there is one other who wishes to speak, very briefly and I am being allowed, very kindly to introduce this gentleman from Russia, the one who was very recently murdered through poisoning, I think he was known as Vladimir, and that is how I am being told to introduce him as Vladimir."

"Well thank you Ghandi, it's been very nice to talk to you."

"Very interesting to try and speak, I think my sheer dogged determination, and I was known for that on the earth plane, has really helped me with this, but it is erm, no disrespect, but I shall be quite glad to return to the spirit world as it is so much lighter, but I has been nice to speak to you. So I will step back as I think Vladimir is ready to speak to you now."

"Thank you."

With that Ghandi, or whoever our confused communicator was, had gone, and I waited to speak to this mysterious Vladimir character.

****

"Good evening," I said, realising that another personality had stepped into John's energy to speak with me.

A firm and very powerful voice said with quite a pronounced Russian accent "Good evening!"

"It is very interesting to speak to you."

"You know the President Putin, he think he could shut me up, but he cannot, as you quite rightly say, we can speak from the Spirit world."

"Absolutely!"

"Well, the finger of accusation, not even of suspicion, but of accusation, I identify President Putin as the man behind my assassination. It was on his direct orders that I be taken out."

Assuming incorrectly I was talking to Alexander Litvinenko I commented, "What a horrible way, what a really nasty way, to be ill and die like that!"

"Not pleasant, but you have to understand that in the business that I was engaged in, these sort of things were not as rare as you would think, just some are not so easy to cover up as others. You have a joke, you say about doctors burying their mistakes."

"Yes, or isn't it dead doctors don't lie or something?"

"All are true as well, there are very many ways that secret agents can kill an individual and make it look as if it was erm heart failure, accident, and it is not just your own country that has these sort of activities going on, and it is no secret that these things go on. What people also need to understand is that sometimes there are very corrupt people whose desperation to cling to power, wherever that may be in the world, will go to any lengths to ensure that they get what they want. I am not sad or even angry that I have been killed, I took it to be part of my possible reward for the work I was doing. You do not become an agent without realising very fully the risk and the very possible outcome of your untimely death. But the idea was obviously not just to take me out, it was also to send a signal to others…"

"Do not mess with us?"

"Exactly, do not mess with the Russian President, and this is the pain and anguish you will endure if you dare to speak out. Well he cannot poison me now, and even if he were to try and kill every medium on the planet, he will not stop me speaking out and indicating him as the man who had me murdered."

"Well I hope Vladimir that that does not incriminate John and me, and we get poisoned as well, you'd better protect us okay?"

"He will not dare to do this now, because if anything was to happen to either of you, then anybody on the planet who will have read what you have written, will very immediately, rightly or wrongly, will jump to the conclusion that you were taken out by unseen forces, so it is in the interests really of security services around the world that the two of you should live to be very old people."

"We hope so!"

"I do not think that you have anything to worry about."

"No, we're not really worried."

"I wish the Russian people to know, what their leaders arrange and command just so that they can possibly cling to power."

"Is there anyone else in danger at the moment Vladimir?"

"I do not say anything, because there are others who could be at risk. Whilst I can say these things with you, I am very aware because of the work that I was engaged in that it is so easy to take someone out and make it look, as I say, heart failure, natural causes, whatever you like, and I have no wish to put anyone at risk at this present time. If needs be I will quite gladly give information, so I say this to President Putin, be warned because Vladimir will find his revenge!"

At this point our tape ran out so I had to ask Vladimir to wait so I could capture all the relevant detail of our conversation. I continued by saying, "It's alright now, do you understand that we are taping this?"

To which Vladimir nodded affirmatively, then he once again spoke to me. "You know, just to give a little further evidence that it is I who is speaking."

"Yes, that would be really helpful."

"Which I think is important, there are witnesses to the way that my apartment in Moscow was completely turned upside down, in fact there is still information, which they are trying to find, but it is so well hidden…"

"They are not going to find it?"

"No, they will not find it, but when the time is right, even from beyond the grave I will reveal the source of that information, and it will be published, and it will be, well, shall I say I shall be very delighted to see the faces of certain people when it is published."

"And will this be the sequel do you think Vladimir?"

"Sequel?"

"This is the first book that we are writing, there will be another book that we will write?"

"I do not know, I just was asked if I would say a few words on this subject. Again it is all as a friend was just saying, that to make the people of your world understand that this is not isolated in one country this sort of activity is constantly taking place around the world. Your people live in ignorance of what is done, and it is time that the people rose up and said 'enough'! We want justice, and we want peace, fighting and killing needs to stop."

"Yes! I agree with you wholeheartedly."

"And those who are guilty of mass murder need to be exposed for the villains that they really are!"

"You speak with great passion Vladimir!"

"Well you could say, I am very angry, and I am! But not so much for myself, but I was passionate for my country, and passionate that the best for our country should be done. It is not being done now, and it is being manipulated and being pushed towards ways that will not benefit the people of Russia and its closely surrounding countries and neighbours, it is not good!!"

"I think that's very clear Vladimir, I think that people will be able to understand the clarity in the words that you use."

"Well, I am being instructed, I suppose in one way I was good at taking instructions, but I am being told that I need to step away, but I will come back if you would like me to, because I think there is more that we can talk about and there is more I would like to say, because you have a saying in England of 'putting the cat amongst the pigeons', I would very much like to be that cat, and I will do my best to make people aware of what is going on."

"I like your passion and I love your determination, and although you are no longer here on the earth plane you are still working for your cause of your people and the world, and I think that is very important."

"I will make a promise to the Russian people, I will continue to fight for what is right for the people of our beloved country, and I will stand up, and I will continue to say to those who defy and abuse their position of authority, I will expose them for what they are!!"

"Well, thank you very much for coming and talking, it has been very interesting to talk to you. Bless you."

"Interesting words, but I will speak with you again, but I must withdraw."

****

With those words Vladimir departed, and I was quickly joined by the uplifting presence of Jimmy Jones.

"Hi Jimmy!"

" Hiya."

"One very determined man eh? Very determined!"

"He's phew! His energy's very strong, he's a nice guy actually, but, phew, that blew me away, well it's all part of the jigsaw puzzle coming together slowly and just a couple of more pieces in the jigsaw puzzle we can build up here. Well I guess we've taken up enough of your time for now, and I wasn't sure if I was going to be able to come back at all."

"Is that to do with time restraints or is it to do with John?

"Well it's him, isn't it, if he's being a pain in the backside then we have to come away more quickly. He's behaving himself a bit tonight! Anyway I will disappear now, when we come back again I will bring some others for you as well."

Jimmy then withdrew, and John then started to come back. It had been a very long session, but certainly an interesting one. Afterwards we did some research only to discover that certain facts with regards to Ghandi were incorrect, and secondly to discover that I had not been talking to Alexander Litvinenko but a second Russian spy who we only know as Vladimir.

We wondered if things could become clearer in the course of our next sitting. As if things couldn't get more interesting, we were soon to be shown how much more interesting they would become.

11 ALEXANDER AND GHANDI

Our next sitting commenced with Chin Lee stepping forward and speaking to me.

"I am only here just for a brief moment, I am to hand over to young Jimmy, who wishes to address you, my job is to make sure as usual that everything is balanced and controlled and I shall be observing from the sidelines. So again child, have a very good conversation and I will speak to you again soon."

"Okay thanks Chin Lee."

A few moments passed and I was once again joined by Jimmy.

"Hi Jimmy."

"How are you?"

"I have a sore tongue today, under my tongue like an ulcer."

"Poor you, sore tongue eh? You know where we was in the trenches you'd be hard pushed sometimes just to get a drink of water, and your tongue would stick to the roof of your mouth. Your feet would swell up so bad, you'd daren't take your boots off cos you wouldn't get em back on again."

"That's awful!"

"Yes, well it was a long time ago. I'm sure it <Susan's tongue> will be better soon."

"Hey, that was interesting the other day wasn't it?"

"Yes it was interesting, but we do have some questions though."

"Well maybe I can help you out a bit before you start asking questions eh? I thought it was quite funny actually I was having a right laugh, cos you two had jumped to a conclusion as to who the Russian fella was, I think you can actually understand he is someone different although he's connected with the one you were thinking about. There is another one here who wishes to talk to you about the same thing, and also, well we'll have to see about that Mr Ghandi."

"Well he wasn't the Ghandi we were thinking about."

"Two people there, you know that connect with different things, well you could blend your mind to think they blend with different things, but they don't."

"Is that all part of the plan?"

"Well of course, remember what we said this book is not just about bringing some people forward, it's also getting people to understand the difficulties in communication, and you know, there are a load of Jimmy Browns and Jimmy Jones and all sorts of, as some people would say common names. So it didn't make sense that someone who presented themselves as Jimmy Jones to you, might not be me! I am just one of the many ain't I. Equally we might be talking about one hot subject like we know this, the er, poisoning of that poor Russian chap…"

"Alex?"

"Well see, you got it wrong again haven't ya. Well Alex was one of them who was poisoned, but I was talking about Vladimir."

"Oh! Vladimir who we were talking to, yeah."

"Vladimir was the Russian. Anyway it just shows you how easy it is to be confused over who is talking and what they are talking about, and even if they are talking about the same subject it's easy to assume you are talking to one person when you are actually talking to someone else. We have the gentleman here, who you really thought you was talking about, would like to talk this evening. You can call him Alex, he doesn't mind you calling him Alex, it wasn't his full name, but that's how he likes to er, well that's how he likes us to call him over here. So you call him Alex ok? Just listen to what he's got to say but don't forget obviously with all your questions. Before I hand over have you got anything else you'd like to ask me about or have I covered everything?"

"I think you have covered everything that we need, but I suppose one of the things that bothers John and I have been talking about is that it all feels a bit too amazing, really you know, to feel that I am talking to these people and the whole controversy of it all."

"I can understand how people on the earth plane will find it hard to believe, but when you think about where I was in the First World War, and there we were fighting in the most awful conditions, yet the people back in England, they were led to believe that we were on some victorious war, that was full of glory and courage and valour. Well there was a lot of courage and valour, but it wasn't all the painted picture it was made out to be. I think sometimes people get a completely distorted view of what reality is on the ground. So I can understand that to some people that it might seem really weird, why would these people come and talk. People are quite happy to go around their daily lives believing that everything is quite all right, when there are in some cases, things going on that they would be horrified about. That's why we have decided to come together to let people know that there are these things going on. That there are people willing to do things that most people would consider, I don't want to say evil, but bad things that go against the common good of everyone, and they are willing to do that for a price and are willing to sell their brother and sister to do that."

"I think we also feel that we are going to make a lot of people very unhappy about this book, and we are selfishly thinking of ourselves, and obviously the family we wish to have."

"What I can tell you, is that you will all be okay, not just you two, but the extended family will be fine as well. Don't forget we didn't enter into this lightly, and we will do everything to make sure you are kept safe. Some people will be quite upset, of course they will, but they are criminals and criminals don't like being found out."

"We wondered whether this was also part of our path, to write this book, but also maybe, give our lives for it as well?"

"Well you're not as such going to give your lives for it, that's not going to be allowed to happen. But in another way you could say you are giving your lives to it."

"I mean in losing our lives on the earth plane."

"In another way you would be losing your life because you're going to be so busy with people wanting to talk to you and wanting to interview you and stuff like that, and you will find that the publicity that is drawn from it people will begin to recognise you down the street, but you will be fine, we will be with you every step of the way. You will find that even after the book is written, those of us involved are intent on being around you when you are talking about all these things, so that we can keep giving you our influence and words and questions that might come up, maybe we can give you another answer that might be of use to the people who want to listen. Don't worry we will be with you every step of the way. Everything will be fine. Well I am going to step back because I know this Alex is ready to talk We'll let him come forward and have a chat with you, and you can ask him what you like, but as I say this is the man you thought you were talking to. Vladimir is here as well, he is listening."

"Did he have a laugh?"

"Well, you know he's not one for laughing, I have to be nice cos he's standing right here. He feels very strongly and passionately about what's gone on, he knows, he does know who is responsible, and he holds them very personally responsible. Well you heard what he said so I don't really need to say anymore. But he's listening here as well so I am sure he's helping Alex with this, well let's see what they say. Well I'll be back to speak to you, but don't worry everything will be okay."

Jimmy withdrew, and Alexander Litvinenko drew close and we began our next interview.

"Good evening," I said. "Can you give me your full name?"

"Alexander."

"And your second name?"

I was met with silence and presumed I was not going to be given the answer I was looking for so asked. "Are you not going to tell me?"

"No."

"Why don't you want to say?"

"In my line of work, that was not considered a good thing to talk and use too much of your own personal information. Everything is secretive, but people will know who I am. I was a very stubborn man."

"And you still are?"

"Still stubborn and very determined as well and I am so delighted in a way to speak from this existence, this world where we exist. Of which I had little knowledge of before coming here."

"Have you been here before, talking through an instrument?"

"Not in this way, but I have been trying to impress thoughts on people they tell me are sensitive, but this is different."

"That's okay, you can just take your time."

"Let me talk about what happened to me, and why I was despatched in the way that I was. In the world of espionage and secret services, it is quite common practice to remove people who are considered a liability. Because I was willing to speak out about President Putin and those who served him, I was considered to be a liability that must be removed, which is why that came to be. It is very obvious to everyone I do not need to talk, or say I was murdered, it is obvious that was the case. The question in many people's minds is who is responsible. You know it is something I did not actually dream of when I was dying, I knew I would not live, because I was so very, very ill. But I did not think I would have the opportunity to speak from the Spirit World. I have not been here very long and am still trying to understand everything. I remember saying that I would not be silenced, and isn't it great that I can speak from here, and those that tried to silence me cannot do a thing about it now."

"It's fantastic that you can speak your truth."

"There is great danger for the people of the lands to where you call Eastern Europe. There is a desperate struggle taking place within the Kremlin, and indeed within the former Soviet states, there is a big power struggle taking place. President Putin is being quite ruthless in maintaining his power base. He has ordered the removal of several former agents, both of the KGB and FBS, because they were discovering information that would personally incriminate him and some of his colleagues. I was about to reveal a report on matters of state security, and that meant touching on the death of a colleague. There is someone can be bothered amongst the press to match the details amongst several journalists and agents that have mysteriously disappeared, they will discover there is quite a connection between all of these things but a very clever attempt also to cover them up to make them look as if they are individual events rather than clearly connected direct to the secret services of Russia. But it is the Russian secret services under the instruction of President Putin who have carried out these monstrosities. It is time that the people of the rest of the civilised world that one of the biggest countries of the world has as its leader one of the worst terrorists you could have.

"It is time he was removed for the benefit of the Russian people and the people of the surrounding states especially Georgia and Chechnya who have suffered quite terribly as a result of his march for power."

"How long has he been in power?"

"He is on his second term of office, I cannot remember exactly how far into it he is, but in terms of being in power, you do not have to be in an office to have power. He was involved in many things before he was even elected as President. There was a lot of, I think you would say, backdoor activity taking place. Deals being done behind closed doors, which he had a hand in. Which is also how he managed to get elected in the first place. That he was helped and promoted by certain influential people, who used their economic strength to encourage people to elect him.

The proper counter is being very carefully handled so he is given the best possible image in his own country. But the reality is actually quite different. My concern is not for him, but for the people of the country he is elected to serve, and those that he is trying to literally beat with a stick. I am not particularly bitter about the way I passed."

"Although it was a very painful way."

"In terms of the physical, it was not pleasant at all. It at least afforded me the opportunity to say some very clear statements before passing away."

"They chose a very sinister way to kill you."

"It was a very foolish way too. If they had done it in one of the Russian states or something, they could have possibly covered it up, but in your country, the options are not so easy for them, it's not impossible to cover up, but it is much, much more difficult because of the services and the police forces in the former Soviet Union are riddled with those of criminal intent. It is not the same in your country. The vast majority of your policemen are actually decent, hardworking people who abide by the laws they are employed to uphold, something you should be proud of in your country."

"Does that also include MI5 and MI6?"

"Well they are a different breed altogether and they are of like, and some people are going to be very upset by what I say, but they are using the same tactics that every other secret service in the world uses and I don't think that is a major surprise to the public at large, all of them will use methods to dispose of people in ways that serve the state as it is, as it wishes to be served at the time. If they dare to speak out about what they have done, then they themselves are removed. It happens across the world."

"I think that the majority of people are not aware of this, I think they may have an inkling that some things happen underground, but they don't know the full extent of it."

"I think the other thing that is important to understand is that whilst you may have the odd one or two who are in a very senior position who abuse that power in truth across the world, the vast majority of the abuse of power is people of lesser position, not necessarily those in the top position. Unfortunately in Russia it is different, but in the rest of the world, largely speaking it is the lower ranks who are more corrupt and open to criminal activity, and sometimes it is not because of political reasoning, but just even for personal gain or personal reasons so you know that they wish to pursue their own agendas."

Alex had struggled over the last part of his conversation, so I asked, "Are you finding it a difficult to stay here, focussed?"

"You know for someone who was very well versed in paying attention, this method of communication requires a great deal of concentration. I suppose there will be some that will say well he didn't concentrate very well if he managed to get poisoned!"

"How was it done Alex?"

"It was within the fish or a drink that was provided."

"Was it Sushi?"

"Yes, either the fish or a drink, and I fell for the oldest trick in the book, my attention was diverted for a second, and that is all that is needed to be able to plant any sort of poison."

"Would this have been prepared in the kitchens?"

"No, no, it is not the staff in the kitchens that need to be scrutinised, they are the unfortunate victims and unfortunately they were very closely looked at. It is a very simple act to actually poison a drink or poison food, all you need is a few seconds of distraction."

"Is it a liquid or a powder?"

"In this particular case it was administered in a more liquefied form. The trouble is as well with these things, a lot of the time they are tasteless. I remember thinking that the fish tasted a little bit odd…"

"Well sushi can be a bit like that?

"Exactly, because of all the spices and everything, and it's easy to have digested, and before you can think about it the damage has been done."

"Does it happen instantly Alex?"

"The poison that was used is very toxic, but very carefully administered, so that just the right amount was given so that I would have longer to live than needed to be. It was not a humane way of dispatching someone."

"Does it affect your organs, your vital organs?"

"In effect all the organs in turn shut down and the damage is irreparable, and depending on the dose depends on how quickly that happens. I was pleased to stay awake and conscious for a few days."

"I remember seeing newspaper pictures of you and media attention about it, it was pretty awful. Is there anything else you would like to say about it?"

"There are things I feel I would like to reveal, but I am not sure we need to do this right at this moment. What I think will be interesting, because some people will say much of what he has spoken about we already know, what I think I would like to do, I think it will help add weight to the conversations you have had, is to help inspire both of you when you are given the opportunity to be interviewed. So that we can give some more specific information that we can rattle the cages a little bit further."

"You don't think it's appropriate to say it now?"

"Why forewarn those who you could very quickly and publicly announce as being criminals if we put it in the book right away? It gives those who support these activities to create cover stories. I would prefer if it is okay, to speak later as you say on the thought level. I can help you both when you are asked questions about my conversation and connection."

"Well we trust that that will be the right way."

"Well I am also under instruction here, that this is probably the best way that we can get it, because we are very concerned that we get the message across of what this sort of corruption does, not just in your country but across the world, and that these people need to be brought to book and if they are very publicly denounced in a way that is not forewarned about, then we can maybe hit home and make sure things are actioned to eliminate as much as possible this sort of activity."

"Okay."

"I think I am going to have to step back, from this I find this is very…to talk through a person, requires me to think very strongly and clearly. I can do that, but the longer I do that the harder it is to maintain my thought processes and I need to pull back."

"Thank you, it's been very interesting."

On our final recording session Alex came to speak to us one final time so we insert his words here as a conclusion to his testimony.

"Good evening Alex."

"Good evening. I think I am supposed to say a few final words. I think I would like to say to people who may read this, that I understand fully that many of you will find it difficult to accept that what has been written is from the words of people that you all consider to be dead. I understand that very clearly because my understanding in life was that when you are dead, you are dead. That is the way of the world that you live in that many consider death as the finality, when of course I know now that it is not. It is just one end of one phase and the beginning of another."

"Yes."

"We have given you some very interesting information. Some of which will be of great interest to some, some will have been of greater interest to others. I talk about particularly those not necessarily directly involved in your secret services or the secret services of other nations, but those that operate behind them, that use those agencies as cover for their own work. It is not necessarily governed and sanctioned by government agencies, but they use the government agencies as cover for their nefarious activities. I don't wish to dwell on that. I think suffice in what has been said already is enough. What I would say to people is to think very carefully, if just one part of this information from the very many people involved is proven to be true and correct, then you must also consider that what has come from the rest of us is true and correct. That we have come close to the earth plain to let our fellow human beings be aware of what is being done in their name, sometimes completely without their knowledge and certainly without their consent. It is time for the people of the earth to be aware of all these activities and to start to ask relevant questions and bring these people to account for their activities which are purely based around materiality, greed, financial aspects and very rarely for the very best causes of all of mankind even in one country or another. I just hope that people will read what has been said and give some consideration to what has been said, and just be aware of the possibilities that what they have been told is the truth from those that have spoken it."

"I was just going to say, even if people don't believe all of it, I think there will be a knowing that this could actually be true."

"What I have been told is that all people, even if they believe themselves to be not psychic in anyway at all, but when they are faced with truth, it does resonate within, there is a knowing of what is right and what is wrong. I think that many people will feel that resonation within themselves that we have said is the truth and something they should give due consideration to."

"I think that's right Alex, and I think no matter what walk of life you are from, and for whatever reason you have decided to read this book, I think there will be aspects that will resonate even if some of it doesn't."

"I think also a very relevant point is that very much what has been spoken about has been about what has happened within the United Kingdom and the Russian Federation, but what has been said applies to every other government or state on this planet, and that the people of all the countries need to be aware that things take place that they would be horrified to understand are taking place in their country. That is why we are very intent that people know and hear the truth and understand that these agencies or groups exist, and that they should now be pulled to account and prevented from any further activities that undermine not only the lives of every man woman and child, not only undermining every politician and local representative of the people, it undermines the humanity of mankind itself. That is what we are intent of making people aware of and helping them to bring an end to this totally unnecessary activity."

****

Alex's final words for now had been spoken; Jimmy Jones stepped into the fray to share his thoughts with us.

"Is that Jimmy? That was interesting"

"You knew it was me! Yeah interesting. Interesting for us listening as well, just even watching Alex trying to get his thoughts into alignment with John, that was interesting as well, and trying to get his thoughts across. I agree with him, I think that it's best that he keeps some of that more detailed information that he can feed you when you are given an opportunity to talk on the radio or in front of the TV cameras, we'll maybe give some very detailed information then. Our intention is not for this just to be considered some sort of lightweight book that people can knock off as entertainment. It's to let people know we are who we say we are, and we have a very serious message to bring to the people of the earth, and for them to be aware of what's being done, and sometimes in their name, and sometimes definitely not in their name, but it needs to be addressed for your earth plane to be safe. Especially those who are in a position of power well, they need to be sorted out, they can't be allowed to do this. It's very dangerous to have people of criminal intent in charge of things that could be dangerous."

"Are you needing to pull back?"

"Is there anything you want to ask, has it all been clear enough?"

"Yes, it's all been clear thank you, is Ghandi not coming back today?"

"He's around, he's around, hang on a minute, lets see if he wants to <lose sound here> he's is standing over here, well both of them."

"Both of them? What do you mean both of them?"

"Two Ghandis. Would you know, I think the one you thought you would be talking to, they call him Mahatma Ghandi, that's different from the other one. In a way we were playing a bit of a game with you guys."

"Well we kind of realise that now."

"Because there were Maha…maha… cor that's a mouthful innit?"

"Mahatma Ghandi."

"Yes, that's a mouthful that is. Anyway he was also trying to give you bits, and other bits were sort of distorted."

"That was the thing, all the dates and things like that, some of it matched and some of it didn't."

"Well let's see if we can help sort some of that out. Let's give it a go, we'll get Mahatma, I'm not going to say Ghandi, we'll ask him if he can come and have a little chat."

"Okay."

Jimmy stepped back and a short time later Mahatma Ghandi came to speak, I hope this time without any distortions.

I greeted our latest communicator with, "Good evening there."

"Hello. I am very sorry for the confusion we caused you the other day. It was a sort of double experiment of dealing with the confusion that arises sometimes in communication, which some people will love to have conversation and discussions about. But I think it's also important maybe for those who are sensitive who work with what you do to maybe understand that they think they are talking to one individual, and they could have two talking at the same time."

"We realise that now."

"As you know I was the subject of several assassination attempts."

"Yes, we do know that now, because we have researched it."

"I was never going to be put off by people trying to intimidate me by taking my life. I am sure actually they weren't trying to intimidate me, they were trying to kill me, but when they failed obviously, one just picked yourself up and carried on with the work, because it was so important that we carried on the fight for our country, but there were some who would just not tolerate my say, my line of thought, and others had their own line of thought, and I guess you can say these sort of things happen. What can I say about the confusion? The other gentleman, who also shares the name of Ghandi, is not in fact actually related to myself or the other quite famous Ghandi family. But Ghandi is a well-known name and people will assume, and even some who are terrorists can make a mistake as well, and they will find a name and think this is a relative of this person and take action against them. But of course those sorts of things are not necessarily as well recorded and there was this gentleman with the unfortunate surname of Ghandi, they tried to kill him with a roadside bomb thinking he was a relative of mine, when he was not. Again unfortunately for him he lived in the New Delhi area as well, it really was a case of mistaken identity and one could say an attempt to apply pressure on the Ghandi family at large to step away from politics. It is a matter of great sadness for me that other people were victimised in that way."

At this point our tape recorder came to the end of the tape, the noise of the tape stopping was enough to disrupt our conversation. However, Ghandi quickly re-established his connection through John. I restarted our conversation apologising for the tape machine stopping so abruptly. Mahatma Ghandi replied;

"It is okay, it has an effect more because it momentarily breaks our mental connection and that's a little bit disconcerting, but it's okay now, it's okay. Yes, I regret people being caught up, just because they happen to share a similar name and live in a similar vicinity. But you also need to understand that in the time of the late 1840s, it was just after the war, there was a still a lots of attempts from people demanding change, and they were pushing those through with violence as well as peaceful means. So some of the events will have been just considered another act of violence, sectarian and the such like, and not necessarily originally associated with myself, and the campaign that I was noted for. I think it may just give an example of how people can be very confused by information and, you know, there will be some that will have read the first bit of this conversation and will say 'Oh there you go, this proves this; and that's not necessarily the case. You can have a mistaken identity, you can have two people from Spirit trying to talk at the same time, and all of those things can add to the confusion and make it more complicated."

"Yes, and we understand that now."

"But um, you know again, there have been many occasions, not just during the course of my life, not just in the course of my personal story, but there have been others who have met with assassinations, and often that has been ascribed to some lunatic or other, or fanatic and that's quite an easy way to write those things off. You know sometimes that isn't really the case. There have been murders supposedly carried out by individuals who are then rapidly despatched themselves. So they cannot speak out later on, who have really just been the fall guy for those who wish to abuse power."

"A bit like a suicide bomber really?"

"It is, but it's backed quite often by state financing, which is the worrying thing for people I think. A lot of general people whilst not being at all happy that terrorists are about and doing those sorts of things have understood that fanatics exist. But to grasp the concept that some of the so-called terrorist acts are carried out with the sanction of those in power is a really worrying thing for the general public. It is not our purpose really to cause widespread panic, which I know will be an accusation thrown out, but it really isn't the case."

"It's an awareness Ghandi."

"It is an awareness, and also for those in power who are genuine people trying to do the very best for their country to actually focus on these issues, and get these real trouble makers out of their system so that the people can really have faith that they are being governed with the very best of intention, and not being the victims themselves of people acting in unlawful ways. I hope I have managed to clear some of that up?"

"Yes, you have thank you. What work are you doing now Ghandi?

"I am obviously still interested in the objects of peace, and I have worked very much for peace in my own country of India, and I look for ways of influencing peace between those of Pakistan and India, and the Kashmere province as well, and use the facilities of mind, thought impressions, to help influence to bring about positive and constructive communication between these groups, rather than the path of destruction or fighting which never really solves anything, just causes more problems. But, yes my focus is on obtaining peace, not only in my own country, I do try and help elsewhere if I can, but obviously my love is still for my country that I was campaigning for."

"Yes, yes I understand, very valuable work."

" I must go, because it is becoming more hard."

"Well thank you very much for coming and talking to me, and to highlight some of the things we needed."

Ghandi then withdrew, and I was briefly joined by Chin Lee, who spoke about how it had been a deliberate act by spirit to bring through confused communications. Given Ghandi's faux pax of referring to the late 1840s in this most recent conversation, when clearly he was referring to the late 1940s, it seemed clearer than ever that people in Spirit, no matter of what rank or status, are still people, with all the frailties that all of us here on earth have.

12 DIANA AND VLADIMIR

As ever our evening began with Chin Lee, who came to set the right conditions for our communicators for the evening.

Our first communicator on this occasion was the delightful Princess Diana.

"Good evening Diana."

"Hello, yes, well, it is something that has grabbed the attention of the public at large. Long have they felt that the passing of Dodi and myself was anything but an accident. Much as the authorities rush to make things fit, it goes against the feeling and awareness of the people that there is something fundamentally wrong with the verdict that is being reached. It is very interesting to observe from our side of life how desperate are the attempts and yet it really doesn't need to be. It is so silly, because those that are trying to now to cover up something are actually not the guilty party, but they are working out of fear because they think that maybe the general public will blame them. What they are really doing, inadvertently, is working to help cover up the acts of miscreants who worked in an unlawful manor. In a way it's quite amusing to watch this silliness and desperation to try and cover up what is clearly something that instead of being covered up should be spoken quite openly about. It should be left to the general public to decide for themselves whether what is being reported and what is felt by them, which one is actually the truth. I wish to talk a little bit about our chauffeur, who was driving obviously when the car crashed and the fact that he was, shall we say, unaccounted for, not just on the day we disappeared from the earth plane, but he himself disappeared on several occasions whilst in our employ, and was regularly, shall we say, feathering his own nest. To ensure that when the time came, he would be well looked after. He was passing information to relevant people and I am sure he meant it quite harmlessly in respect of our safety. I do not believe he was deliberately trying to put our safety at risk, but he was feathering his own nest by feeding information to known contacts, who were therefore then paying him certain sums of money for information received, as to where we would be, where we would be going. This information once available was used by not just those that he spoke to, but was used by others who sought to use that information for the most awful of purposes of course. You know much has been written about the excessive bank balance that he had considering the salary that he was on, and no-one seems to be able to put an explanation in place as to why he should have had such funds in his possession. But again this is part of the stupid acts of some in the establishment trying to distance themselves from the episodes that took place. However by so involving themselves in a cover up, they have unfortunately incriminated themselves into being perceived to be somehow responsible for what actually took place.

"I think this is all very, very important that people understand, that, you know, I am very keen to protect those that were not directly involved. I do think it is rather stupid and foolish of them to then, er having seen that they could possibly be incriminated in some way desperately trying to cover up, and in so doing covering up the tracks of the real miscreants, and indirectly making themselves seen to be much more culpable of the very allegations they have been accused of that they are trying to distance themselves from."

"Well Diana, when you speak today, you speak very, very clearly and it seems to be much easier for you?"

"Every time I speak, although I cannot get used to this man's voice, but every time I do speak and make this contact it is much easier each time. It's a case of once you can learn how to focus your mind into blending with that of whoever it is you are working with then the whole process becomes much easier, and I find it much easier to speak now than when we were first having conversations, which as you remember were quite difficult and strained."

"Have you come through and spoken to anyone else in this way?"

"Not in the way in you are speaking to me right now. Well I suppose that's not completely true, there have been a couple of occasions, but it really was not very effective and I did not feel comfortable so quickly withdrew. However I have contacted several mediums on what you call the 'mental', or others would call the 'thought' level of communication. With varying degrees of success, but this has been the most successful I have been in terms of talking through someone and therefore being a more direct contact. Is there anything else you wish to ask me?"

"I read about Mohammed Al Fayed, and how he is campaigning for all this to come out in the open, it's clear that he is not accepting any of it."

"Well, no of course he won't be, you see not only has Dodi been trying to influence his father, but I have as well, and our combined efforts of impressing into his consciousness that this is not the correct answer, is something that is resonating in his soul level, so he cannot leave this campaign alone. No matter what the outcome or decisions of various faculties involved, he knows that the truth is still yet to come out, and he will continue to fight for both our sakes and for his own peace of mind to find out what the real truth is. Undoubtedly there will be further attempts to cover up what has taken place. Undoubtedly there will be attempts to blacken the names of yourself and er, the young man that I am talking through. Still, on a conscious and soul level those that are sensitive enough will be fully aware that justice is not served by trying to cover up. It is served by telling the truth, no matter how painful that may be. It is far better for the people to know the truth and to therefore come to some understanding than to be fed a pack of lies but still be expected somehow to accept that as being the truth, it just does not go together very well and will not sit very well with the consciences of many people, not just in your country but the countries around the world."

"I guess Diana, one of the things John and I have been thinking about is which type of people are going to read the book, and who would be drawn to it. One of the things we were thinking is that we need some categorical evidence that people will say 'I didn't know that', that they are going to find it interesting for whatever level they are coming at it from?"

At this point I realised that Diana had stepped back from John. I was briefly joined by Chin Lee, who advised me that due to John's health, Diana had been temporarily forced to step back. Having once again settled John, Diana was able to return and continue our conversation.

"Hi Diana."

"Hello again. It is not easy when one suddenly gets thrown out, which is rather funny actually, because it's not something I really experienced when I was on the earth plain, of being thrown out of anywhere. The consciousness of the instrument or medium as you call him, just can throw some anomalies sometimes it is impossible for us to maintain the mental connection. Now I am sorry. You will have to remind me as to where on earth we were with regards our conversation."

"I was asking about the different types of people that may be drawn to this book. So the people that will be interested in you and

Dodi, those interested in the First World War, and others with the Russian connection."

"Well of course they will come from all walks of life. There will be some that, 'regardless whether this is true or not' will enjoy it. There will be others who will say 'Where is the evidence, where is the proof'? and they will not be satisfied, and to be honest even if you were to give them names, dates, places etc, they will say that that is just a cover for something else, and you will not necessarily satisfy those people. But the ones who really need to pay attention are the ones who know quite clearly and categorically that what has been revealed to the two of you is quite true and correct, those are the ones who we really need actually to hit home with our message. We have a very considerable amount of power here, and I don't mean power as in status but a considerable power here in the knowledge that we possess that we can quite easily reveal to the earth plain should we deem it necessary. What we are really seeking here is for these groups who act in such an underhanded way, and in ways that undermine the planet as a whole to be brought back into a more controlled fashion. That these acts of violence against individuals should be stopped, there is no need for that. This is where we aim to hit home, but yes we do understand the difficulties but also you need to understand, and readers need to understand how difficult it is, because if we were to name names and dates, there would be sort of other accusations that clearly we didn't get the information from spirit, but that it was of the earth plain and negate anything that is supposedly said from the spirit world. There will be those that will say 'you cannot speak to the dead, because my experience tells me that when you are dead, you are dead', and they will not accept any other mode of thought. There will be others within what you call the spiritual understanding, that will accept that you have been talking to us individuals, and will also understand quite rightly why you have not been able to, or even been fed very specific detail on some occasions, because of the very dangers of you know, you will be damned if you do, and damned if you don't.

"So we understand how very difficult that is, but we aim to bring out information, I think this was said to you before by someone else, but we aim to bring out information at the time you are interviewed that could be very specific and reveal more detail, in a more live, shall I say, situation, that I think maybe even more relevant than having it just recorded in a book, and also negates that question of preparing the enemy for an attack before it has happened. Therefore we can bring things out into the open, very, very quickly and therefore not allow those that are seeking to undermine society at large the opportunity, of some sort of defence. Does that help a little?"

"Yes, It does help, absolutely."

"We will try and give you some specifics, but it's not necessarily in the best interests to give lots of detailed information quite now for that very reason that I have just spoken about."

"Thanks Diana, that is really helpful."

Diana and I then chatted briefly about William and Harry, much as any mother would talk lovingly about her children. I then asked some personal questions to satisfy my own interest, but very soon we needed to say our farewells. However on our final session which came later, Diana spoke again, as these are her final words to us for this particular book it seems appropriate to enter them here.

Diana Princess of Wales came to speak to us one final time for this book and we chatted in our usual friendly manner.

"Good evening Diana, it's nice to speak to you again."

"I am not quite sure what I need to say."

"What would you like to say?"

"Some things I would like to say on a personal level."

Diana then gave us some private information to give to her two obviously beloved sons. As requested we have refrained from inserting those personal items from this text, suffice to say they were very personal and we respect Diana's request that we will pass those pieces exclusively on to them in person if we ever get the opportunity, she continued.

"For the general public I would like to say that I extend my most grateful thanks for the love and esteem that they held me in. I would also like to say thank you to those who were of support to me in my earthly life.

"To those responsible for the untimely deaths of myself and Dodi, I was never one to threaten anybody, and I do not threaten anybody now, but I will say that the evidence that exists will show you in your true colours and you will be brought to justice and I look forward to the day when that happens.

"To the Royal Family, and this can be published, I feel very saddened that many of you have been slighted by the media and have wrongly been accused of being implicated, or involved in mine and Dodi's demise. You have a great job ahead of all of you, and from where I am in the Spirit world I will do my best to support you in your work for the best interests of the people in the United Kingdom and indeed the world. To the leaders of all the political parties, and this is lovely, because when on earth as a member of the royal family you are not allowed to speak about political matters, that to all the leaders of all the political parties I ask that you conduct your own investigations into what has been spoken about in this book, and seek to find those responsible and bring them to justice. Further I just wish to add that I have a life here in Spirit that I am happy with the surroundings that I am in now, I miss being able to hold my children in my arms, and I miss some of the aspects of the earth plain, but many of them I don't, but I will be around for many, many years, helping and inspiring wherever I may be. Wherever I can be of influence especially to those who seek to help others who lift lives of others less fortunate into the limelight, so that their lot may be made a better one. I shall continue to work in that field of what you call charity because it is so important that those who do not have the help and support are given as much help and support as possible. I shall do my utmost to influence charities as much as I can so that they can go forward to do what is best for the people they seek to look after and take care of."

"That's lovely Diana."

Diana then told us she needs to withdraw and our final session with Diana was over for this book. Going back to the previous session following Diana, I was then once again joined by Chin Lee, who continued the evening's work by re-introducing Vladimir our mysterious murdered Russian, who after a little struggle in controlling John's energy spoke to me.

"I am the one you call Vladimir!"

"Oh Good evening Vladimir."

"I wondered if it was convenient for me to speak with you again?"

"It's fine for me, I hope it's fine for John."

"I spoke very clearly about my condemnation of Vladimir Putin the President of the Russian Federation and his betrayal of the Russian people by his acts of treason, which is exactly what it is when you abuse your power and position and order the execution of those who would dare to cross your path. I do not say what I say to bring revolution or civil unrest within the Russian Federation; I do not do it for that purpose. I do it for the purpose of people understanding what is going on, and in their ignorance they are unaware that there are people, some of whom they would look at with great reverence, and find that actually that they are people abusing their positions of power, but President Putin is not the only one.

"There is much that has been going on within the former Soviet Union that the outside world is not aware of, and I have come tonight to say a few things, some of it is not so much for your writing, but is, as you have requested, part of your insurance, that will help convince those that need to be convinced that what we are saying is true, and that we, those who purport to come from spirit, are who we say we are, and do have the knowledge that could be of great embarrassment to the various states of various countries, not just the former soviet union or the Russian Federation as it is now called, but your own country and to the Americas and to the countries of various places around the world. Let me give you a few things that will help you build up your little insurance package."

"Is this to be included in our writing or to be kept elsewhere Vladimir?"

"It is for you to record, to place elsewhere for your own purposes. You can place in your writing brief details without giving the full details that I give you here."

For obvious reasons we cannot write here what was revealed to us. However in brief details we were advised of secret deals with regards to abuse of nuclear technology. In the detail, names of states involved were revealed to us, and in some cases names of individuals involved also recorded. In many ways we were horrified by what we were told, if ever made public the consequences for the global community could be catastrophic, we have no doubts that what we have been told is true and accurate, what must be a scary thought for all security services around the world is the fact that the dead, including former spies, can come back and reveal details to those who we call mediums.

Having been given some truly amazing information, we were asked to agree a pledge of silence, unless it was felt to be absolutely necessary. This was not an easy pledge to make, yet given the incredible detail, some of which did indeed turn out to be true, we could do nothing more than to agree a vow of silence until such time we either felt it right to reveal, or are instructed by our Spirit friends so to do. We were also given very careful instructions as to where to store this highly sensitive information, which I am pleased to say is now in a very secure place. We were then given advice as to how to answer our own security services, should they approach us asking for details.

Having divulged an absolute plethora of information, Vladimir then advised us that he had been asked to step back to allow another to join us. One of his final comments was as follows:

"It is time that the world leaders were really true world leaders, and not working for their own personal interests, and personal gain."

****

Following Vladimir's departure, I was joined by the ever-present Chin Lee, who set the scene for our next communicator, the wonderful Winston Churchill.

"Good evening Winston."

"Good evening."

"Good evening it's lovely to talk to you."

"Never, in the field of human existence has so much been owed to so many, by so few. Sadly the few, are not those that work in secret undermining society, the few in this case, are those who are prepared to stand up and speak out, and speak in truth about what is said and done by others who profess to speak on their behalf.

"It is a great sadness that so much has been done to cover up activities undertaken by those who seek to undermine society, democracy and the monarchy. It is shameful that in our beloved country that there are those who seek and use faculties that I can only liken to that of a terrorist to undermine this wonderful country."

"Yes, and I can hear the passion when you speak about that."

"It is very much a time for people to stand up and be counted. It is time for the ordinary men and women, not only of Great Britain, but of the world to stand up and say 'enough is enough, we will not tolerate such behaviour and conduct'. Our leaders must lead, they must set the standard for truth, honesty, and they must be seen to be above and beyond those who act in such deplorable ways."

"Absolutely."

Our communication was brought to an end, due to the conditions not remaining suitable for the communicators to maintain their control over John's energy and physical body. Our session was over for this evening, yet still the amazing evidence and wonderful communications, left me with a feeling of excitement. It was as if we were on a roller coaster, and just when you thought you had ridden the best part of the ride, you would turn another corner, and something equally exciting would be awaiting you. I couldn't wait for the next sector of our journey to commence.

13 DODI AND WINSTON

Our first communicator for the evening was our master of ceremonies Chin Lee. We discussed several personal matters and then Chin Lee introduced our next communicator for the evening, Dodi Al Fayed.

"Good evening Dodi."

"Hello. Yes, you know, I am trying again to work with this method, it is a little bit unusual at first, but I think I am getting there. I don't have really very much to say, other than I wish very much for the media, who paid so much attention to myself and Diana to now look very carefully at what has been said, and the words that have been spoken. We wish for them to look at and investigate the truth as we know it to be, of those who sought to bring us down, and again as has been said by others, it is not the royal family that people need to look at, it is others who have sought in their own minds, to do what they believe is right for King and country, but has actually in effect undermined King and country and should therefore hang their heads in shame for the terrible behaviour and conduct that they have pursued in pursuit of their objectives. I know very much that this story, simple as it is, will cause much interest from the media. There is much that will be asked of yourselves. We will also try our very best to rise to the challenge of the questions that come forward, and given the correct journalists making the approach, we will be willing to sit with yourselves and them, for us to speak more directly with the journalists so that we can answer their questions. It is very important for us that what we are doing is seen to be more than see through. It is very important for the journalists not just to accept what has been said but also to check the veracity and clearness, conciseness of everything that we have said. So we are very keen to co-operate as much as we possibly can, which is an unusual turn of events really, because when we were on the earth plane we tried to shun away from them. Here we are now trying to actively encourage them to come and challenge us so that the general public can be aware of the awful things that have been done by others, and the sort of activity that has taken place behind the scenes, not just in your country, but in other countries around the world."

"Dodi, from our point of view we understand the spiritual aspect of what life is, but there will be a lot of people and journalists reading this book who do not have this understanding, and that may think that what we have written is some kind of conspiracy itself. How are we going to get journalists to sit down in front of us, and get John into an altered state so that you or any of the others can talk through him?"

"Remember what we have said, that it will be the journalists who are genuine in their approach who we will work with. We will also be selective of the journalists of who we will choose to work with, and those who we will choose not to work with. Those that are genuinely open-minded, we do not ask for them to be devoted spiritualists, we ask them to be open minded and willing to investigate.

"Those that approach it with reasonable open mindedness we will do everything in our power to co-operate with, and give them the information that they are seeking that they can find on the physical level to corroborate what has been said from the spiritual plain of existence where we live now. I must go now; I hope that has been of interest. I know I will talk to you again, but it will be for the follow up of this story."

We spoke briefly about personal matters relating to Dodi and his father Mohammed, and discussed the possibility of maybe sometime sitting with Mohammed Al Fayed so that his son can speak to him more directly. We hope some day should Mohammed wish to do so, that we can be of service to both him and his father.

Jimmy Jones briefly came to speak and once again to share with us some final thoughts.

"Hi Jimmy!"

"It's been a real pleasure for me, who was just one of many millions who passed in war conditions, it was a delight to be asked to play a part in this book that you are putting together, and to be asked to introduce some of these wonderful characters that I never knew because I'd passed before many of them had come to the earth. Of course Churchill was around, but he wasn't particularly high on my list of personages that I knew of. Anyway it's been a real pleasure to meet these lovely characters and form friendships with them as well, which has been really nice. For someone as ordinary as me it's been a really enlightening experience you know. I have found it fascinating as a layman from this side of life, listening to the story, well you know, it fair blows your mind away, the sort of underhanded things people will get up to. It's really important that people really become aware of it, that there are things going on that ordinary folk need to be aware of, and stop walking around like sheep, and be aware that sometimes some pretty horrible stuff goes on. Sometimes even what they call 'legitimate' government departments some underhanded work goes on, but it's the other totally illegal as you would say, activity, and the governments of the world need to do something about it. After all if you think about the war time conditions, we were fighting for freedom so that all men could live as equals, so that one country couldn't try impose its view and opinion on another. That we could all live truly in peace with each other, and you're still trying to do that right now, on the earth plane. The majority of people just want peace, they want the world to be living as a united whole, yet there are still people in almost every country, intent on looking after their own back pocket more than actually doing what is best for all of the people of the world, and it's such a shame."

Our discussion moved to more personal issues and then Jimmy spoke on the purpose of the book and how it is not meant to be a short term thing of stirring of emotions but to make people look long and hard at what is going on around them. Jimmy also spoke about the world situation and how we need to work to eradicate global issues such as food, shelter, clothing, clean sanitation, as he speaks so clearly on these issues we include it here as it is so relevant even in today's climate.

"Stirring the emotions is not what we are about, we are looking for long term solutions that help people move towards that place where we need them to be. Where they do look to each other, to look after each other, and not to be threatening each other but to be providing food, shelter, clothing and basic essentials that every man woman and child on this planet should have and they aint. We fought in the war for that sort of thing, the First World War and it's still not happening now. There are too many people spending too much money on bombs and all that sort of stuff. What are they spending on creating food for people who are starving? It's a real joke and the leaders of the world should hang their heads in shame. By their neglect they have failed the memories of every man, woman and child who died in all the wars, who fought to bring about true peace, true justice and equality for all."

"If it is true that we choose our parents and we choose our life and we choose what we come to learn, surely there is an element of choosing homelessness and choosing poverty, do you know what I mean?"

"Yes, but there's a big difference between choosing those things and still being forced to not have fresh water. Some of those people have chosen to come for that. Maybe they have come back to highlight the fact that should we not have to live like that, shouldn't we all have the right to drink fresh water, shouldn't we all have proper facilities to deal with bodily waste, shouldn't we all have access to shelter over our heads to keep off the rain or the sun, shouldn't we all have access to wear clothes?"

"I am sure you are right that maybe some people choose to come to that, but I'm not sure they choose it for it to stay that way. I think partly they come, and they do that to show the rest of the world. Stop chasing all your money, all your material things, think about the people in the rest of the world who do not have a thing and are living in absolute dire conditions and it is totally and utterly unnecessary, the world has enough for everybody but it is failing to do it."

"Very strong words from you Jimmy."

"Well, when you've seen the suffering that I have witnessed, when you have seen people willing to give their lives up as I have also witnessed, for causes they think others will pick up after they've gone, and put to rights and then actually find that when it comes to bits of paper being signed, and guns stop firing, that actually their memories are just pushed to one side as if they meant nothing. The aims and objectives and the rhetoric of improvement comes to very little, then we have been failed and we've just been led down a dark path and that's not right, it's not right."

"I hear your words."

"Well I think that's all I've got to say, but we will talk again and I look forward to that. I will bring some other people to you, but that's all for the next chapter as it were, not of this book, but of the ongoing story."

Jimmy then stated he would withdraw and then kindly reintroduced Winston Churchill to me for further conversation.

"Good evening Winston."

"I say this is really very nice for me to come and speak to you. It is a little bit easier for me in some ways to speak to you than I have experienced before. My contact with the medium was very much on the thought level. Speech is something I am very much still trying to get used to."

"It's difficult isn't it?"

"Yes, it is very different, but very interesting to. I was never one to resist a challenge. During the war time years, very much the chiefs of staff would try desperately to prevent me from travelling to where the areas of fighting were still taking place. I would of course have my way, and I would go and show my face to the forces our men fighting out near the front, because it was very important for them to see, that not only did they have the material support behind the scenes at Westminster, but that we would take the steps ourselves to be visibly present where they were, that principally I was not afraid to show my face where the enemy could be nearby, this was very important for the troops involved on all levels. I do not mean just the army, but the navy and air force as well. I should be seen to not only speak from behind the lines but to go to the lines and show my face there as well, so that everybody could be assured that Winston not only supported their efforts with his words, but would actually show his face near to where the action was taking place. This is why in this book it is important for me that I should show my face."

I noticed that whilst speaking to me, Winston spoke with a pronounced lisp even though John did not have one. Winston told me that as it was very much part of his personality that would be recognised, he had chosen to return and speak in this manner. He then continued speaking as follows:

"I was very well known for certain set phrases that I spoke, especially during the war time. In fact many said it was the speeches that I made then, which I mostly would have written exactly as I would have had them said. In other words I didn't have others write my speeches. I said what I felt and knew to be true. I wish to make a final statement.

"The United Kingdom is a country of great significance in the world, it is a world player, it has always been a country that has stood for truth, honesty and for the service of mankind. Never has there been a greater need for the United Kingdom to be a leader in the world, and to be a leader in the path of truth, honesty and integrity. I look to the leaders of the United Kingdom, those who are currently there, and those who are to take over, to always uphold the honour and integrity of this wonderful country that we call our home. One final thing, regarding the young Jimmy Jones; I need to clarify his significance in this entire wonderful story. Jimmy Jones was a soldier who fought and died in World War One. A typical example of the many great soldiers who gave their lives so valiantly in the paths of truth, peace and integrity. When the Second World War was drawn to a close, it was instructed as a normal standard that a broadcast be made, that the secondary group, the ultra secret if you like, resistance group be disbanded. The transmission was to be incorporated in a movie, a newsreel movie, you are too young obviously to have seen those, but in the movie it was movie tone news, were the words 'and at last Jimmy Jones has returned home'!"

I hope Winston will forgive us for finishing with one final well-known phrase that he was recorded as having said.

"This is not the end, it is not even the beginning of the end, but it is most certainly the end of the beginning."